Real Estate Investing For Beginners: Make Money Investing In Real Estate And Generate Passive Income, Wealth & Financial Freedom (With Flipping, Commercial, Rental Property & Realtor Business Ideas)

Author: Jordan Priesley

Table of Content

Introduction

If you are an adult who pays bills, one idea reigns supreme in your mind all the time; it is the thought of how to earn more and become wealthy. We all want to attain a certain level of wealth because it makes it easier for us to do the things we desire. So the question we consistently ask ourselves is this, "How can I make more money?"

While there are numerous businesses, jobs and careers you can utilise to make money, there is one avenue that guarantees timeless wealth you can pass on to future generations. I'm talking about INVESTMENTS IN REAL ESTATE.

The concept of wealth shouldn't be about what you can do to make money for that moment, but how to pool your resources together to guarantee long-term income. So, our focus should be on how to secure more opportunities for passive income.

The objective of this book is to guide beginners through the pathway to get the most out of real estate investment. The chapters and sections you will find below are replete with information that will inspire you to take chances and do more with what you earn.

When the objective of this book is fulfilled, you will experience what it means to be genuinely financially free. Sometimes, economic freedom seems like an illusion for some people who have tried to attain it.

You can enjoy economic freedom in the real estate space if you apply the right principles.

The pathway to the right principles includes an application of this equation: MINDSET + KNOWLEDGE = WEALTH. Knowledge of how to transform your finances combined with a change in mind-set awaits you in the sections you will read through. True lasting wealth is possible; it all begins with the acquisition of knowledge.

The process of investing in real estate goes beyond buying and selling houses; there are many concepts to unbox and learn. It all begins with the first chapter, which focuses on real estate as the pathway to sustainable wealth.

Ready to read through the very first chapter? Head over there now!

Chapter One

Real Estate: The Pathway to Sustainable Wealth

There has been a real estate boom that has caused a lot of people to refocus their attention on the market, and now more people are aware of the authenticity of wealth via real estate proceeds. But, is this boom enough to create sustainable wealth?

When we speak of wealth that is sustainable, we refer to long-lasting and impactful wealth that transcends generations. What else will make for sustainable wealth if not homes and land properties?

Come on, look around you; everywhere you turn, there is a house. We live, survive, and connect based on what we have as properties. The thought of being able to make money off real estate ought to make you extremely excited, because it has great rewards.

More than ever today, more people are attempting to become real estate moguls, and all of them strive to use techniques that will work for them. This has led to a surge in the number of books on real estate. However, it is advisable that you join the wagon with wisdom.

Real estate markets are known for being unstable. As such, every investor (novice or experienced) must become conversant with the principles of successful investing before going ahead with any investment plans.

Without a doubt, the real estate market is beautiful, because when you do make a profit over outstanding sales, it is always a good one. Unlike other sectors in which you may be unsure about the status of your investment despite challenging times, one thing is sure; properties always sell!

So, if you invest in some properties, it is possible to hold off on selling them until you find the right buyer who offers a great price. Should anything happen to a property or investor (accidents or death), the family of that investor can reap a neat profit from the property or pass it on to future generations.

I want you to know that you are on the right path in your search for true, lasting wealth. But, there is a lot of work to be done and many concepts to learn, first.

I always like to share the story of Zuri, a close friend who utilised the ideas shared in this book to make her first real estate investment move. At the time Zuri implemented what she learned, this book wasn't even in print; I just shared the ideas with her and boom! - she put them to work.

Zuri had to follow through with all the ideas we had discussed. She recognised the importance of matching the ideas with actions (which is so essential). And, five years later, Zuri is the proud owner of 12 properties.

I know you are imagining how much she's going to make already with twelve properties, but the number of features isn't the main attraction with this story. What I love about Zuri's story is the fact that she was able to turn those action plans into a success story. It really wouldn't matter if it were just one property she secured; what matters is the fact that with focus and a determined mind, she achieved and surpassed her goals.

So - why real estate? Why should anyone rely on real estate as a source of passive income? Read on to get answers.

The Benefits of Real Estate for Wealth Creation

1.   It is a sure means for passive income.
Passive income is money you gain without having to go to work every day; it is money you don't actively work for. As such, it is the best form of income anyone could aspire to enjoy. You are not considered wealthy until you have a lot of avenues for passive income.

Wealth shouldn't be something you struggle to achieve, nor should it be something that makes you work too hard. You should just put in the work, and it should yield the right results; this is what real estate offers you.

2. Properties always appreciate.
Regardless of how challenging it will be, properties will still appreciate. This is one advantage of real estate investment that makes it very appealing. Zuri isn't bothered about the state of her properties because she knows that whenever she is ready to sell, she will make a profit.

Several investment platforms have a cloud of uncertainty around them; their volatile nature makes it increasingly difficult for people to enjoy the dividends of their investments. An excellent example of such uncertain investments is stocks and shares. But with real estate, you won't have to deal with such issues - especially now that you have this definitive guide with you.

3. Diversification leads to stability.
Real estate diversifies your investment portfolio. This is good, but what is even more interesting is the fact that it can also lead to security in your collection.

When you become an investor, you shouldn't seek assets in just one sector; you can diversify and do more with what you have through various channels.

With real estate, your portfolio is broadened. You experience stability, because when other investments are unstable, your properties bring in a balance that strengthens the portfolio. This feature of real estate investment is crucial to wealth creation.

4. Increased cash flows.

Due to increase in values, your cash flows will also experience the same growth. You have the choice to increase prices on your property and match it up with the current price in the market, and this gives you access to cash whenever you want it.

In a chapter ahead, we will be dealing with the concept of being a landlord. That chapter throws further insight into how real estate aids cash flow. Before we get to that section, you should know that real estate investments will increase your cash flow.

5. Title ownership.

With real estate investment, you also get to enjoy the title ownership of properties. You OWN the properties and decide what you want to do with them. Some people get into severe financial trouble and search for assets to sell off to fix their issues. Yet, because they do not own anything, they are unable to help themselves.

If you invest in real estate, you will have an opportunity to win something that increases in value over time. The most remarkable feeling that wealth gives you is the knowledge of being able to get what you need when you need it; this is a summary of how valuable real estate can be.

6. Transferrable wealth.

Some investments are not transferrable; and this has enormous implications for people who want to invest for their families, spouses, kids, and other third parties.

However, real estate is transferrable. That means you can invest today and transfer the property with its value to another person. It is safe to say that investment in real estate is the gift that keeps on giving; it is a perfect gift idea for someone you love.

More importantly, the fact that it is transferrable also means you can create a legacy of wealth others can build on for a very long time.

7. Tax benefits.

It is possible to get tax deductions on your mortgage interest as you invest in real estate. The tax deductions also apply to cash flows from investment properties, operating expenses, and costs. Insurance and depreciation are not left out in tax deductions.

So, when you start investing, you might want to wrap up all your deals before the year runs out. The end of the year is always a busy time for real estate, as it is an opportunity to utilise all the tax benefits.

With investments in real estate, there are no actual losses; you may have the occasional experiences that every investor has with a stake, but there is one sure thing; you will make a profit.

Over the years, the real estate industry has grown in value as everyone is trying to get their hands on it. You have reached the advantage over everyone else because you are armed with the right tools, knowledge, and information on how this works. So, be prepared to win and get ready to achieve a whole lot with this book.

Since there is an ever-increasing appeal with the real estate market, so many people jump right in and expect instantaneous results. When the results don't pour in as expected, they become frustrated and term the real estate sector "DIFFICULT." Well, I don't think Zuri would have made the kind of progress she did if she had not been patient. Five years is a long time - and Zuri had to wait.

So, in a bid to show you the importance of waiting, we will be heading right over to the next chapter, which will teach you all about the pitfalls of the "get-rich-quick" approach. It is an enlightening chapter that will lead us right into the central conversations of how to invest and succeed with real estate.

Chapter Two

Avoiding the "Get-Rich-Quick" Approach

Lasting wealth takes time to grow; every successful person who shares their story with you will tell you that it took a lot of time for them to arrive at the level of success they now enjoy. The same principle applies to real estate investment.

If you are going to reap the rewards of this approach to investment, then you must get rid of the "get-rich-quick" method. In this chapter, we will consider what the approach is and proffer solutions on how you can be refocused on your investment goals without expecting instant results.

For a person to build wealth quickly, they must do things slowly. There has to be a process of thinking before action is taken. This process helps you weigh all options, thus clearing the pathway for increased success with your investment.

A lot of investors are lured into real estate because they see how many other people excel at it; what they fail to recognise and apply is the fact that these successful people invest an equal amount of time and effort to ensuring that they accomplish their set goals.

For some other successful investors, it was just pure luck.

So if you are considering winning with your real estate investment portfolio, you have to be ready to work on it long term. Those who try to achieve success at once are often disappointed, frustrated, and lose the motivation to continue with their investment.

Simply put - there are no shortcuts to succeeding with real estate. You must imbibe two principles for long-term success; and they are **patience** and **hard work**. Some investors learn a new trick and instantly want to use it to reach the peak. After a few weeks, they realise it won't work and must start all over again.

Some other investors observe a pattern of successful investors and apply it, albeit in a common way. The point is, if you do not put in the same effort, you will not get the same results. The sooner you get the idea of "get-rich-quick" out of your mind, the better off you'll be.

Real estate is like weight loss; everyone talks about it, a lot of people try to make it work, but only a few experience the effects of weight loss. There are millions of people in the real estate and weight loss industry, but only a few get to the peak.

With weight loss, you are told to do straightforward things such as exercise and eat fruits and vegetables, yet the process itself isn't simple. Anyone who has tried to lose weight will tell you it is a serious challenge; it is so severe that some people give up midway into their weight loss programs. In the midst of the struggle, some people come on television to testify about the effect of the process in their lives.

So, sitting in your home and watching those testimonials will cause you to wonder if there is something you are doing wrong. The weight loss experience isn't a fraudulent one; you are just not putting in the required effort and work needed; and until you do, your weight will be a struggle.

Too many people are impatient; it is the reason they don't get the results they seek. If you are serious about losing weight, the same way you are passionate about succeeding in real estate, you will follow through with the process regardless of how long it takes.

There are some steps you can take toward ensuring that your philosophy about real estate doesn't deviate to the "get-rich-quick" pattern. Below, you will find the steps you should consider.

How to Achieve Real Estate Investment Plans

1.   Set realistic goals.
First, you must have goals. For anything significant to succeed, you must have a plan - and your goals form the springboard of your projects. So, if you are prepared to succeed, you have to sit still and curate

plans that focus on how you want to execute your real estate business.

With your goals in hand, you will have a compass that drives and propels you forward - even in challenging times. Before you launch out to begin your real estate adventure, take the time to set goals.

2.   Work hard.

Now, the importance of this cannot be overemphasised. You must work hard to ensure that your goals come to fruition. Your goals give you the motivation you hope for the future, but hard work is what makes a dream come true.

Every day, do something that takes you closer to the realisation of your goals. For every effort you make, you will be rewarded with success. So, work hard and put in your best work toward your goals.

3.   Be patient.

As you curate goals and work hard, remember to exercise patience. Do not be in a hurry to get results, because impatience makes people miss out on something good. You should imbibe the culture of tolerance that enables you to hold on to something until it works out for you.

Tell yourself you are not going to give up until the results start to trickle in. An investor who wants to succeed must be patient; this is a rule that is true of all investment sectors.

4. Focus on quality, not quantity.

A lot of times, investors are in a hurry to excel. As such, they start buying properties. Oh! They buy a lot of features in a bid to show how "successful" they are. Going for quantity over quality is always the wrong approach.

Instead of buying many properties that aren't valuable, it is advisable that you stick with quality over quantity. It is better to have one house that is an asset positioned to increase in value within a specified period than have several properties that are undervalued. Always remember this; stick to quality over quantity.

5. Education + action = success.

Next, you need to educate yourself on the principles and steps to take for successful real estate investment. However, education is not enough; it is crucial that you match your education with actionable steps.

Education + action is the combination that leads to success as a real estate investor. So as much as you are committed to learning, be focused on acting as well. Everything you read, starting with this book, should come to life and work for you.

6. Continue learning

You must continue learning so you always have ways through which you can stay motivated and forget about the "get-rich-quick" pattern. If you had not read this book, you probably wouldn't have gotten all of the ideas you have now.

Read more books and continue to inspire yourself with words and plans. Books, mailing lists, podcasts, etc. are all avenues for learning you can utilize.

7. Aspire and emulate.
Don't just look up to others; make up your mind that you are going to be like them. So first, you must develop the aspirations to be like the successful investors you see - and then emulate them by putting in the same kind of work they put into their investments.

The pattern to success doesn't end with aspirations alone; act, fail, learn, fail, and continue until it is perfected.

8. Observe the trends.
Trends help us decipher what is working and what isn't. You must observe the real estate market, the same way you track your shares and stocks.

By not observing trends, you will be listening to speculations from non-investors - or unprofessional ones who want to get instant cash. Follow the pattern by following other original investors like yourself; you will get to know what's happening within seconds.

9.   Avoid magic bullets.
Magic bullets refer to quick fixes people look for to succeed; they are not the steps that lead to sustainable wealth, nor are they the approaches that will lead to long-term success.

Magic bullets will make it difficult for you to see the bigger picture. As such, they must be avoided at all costs. Magic bullets make it all seem very easy; but in no time, it will come crashing down on you.

10.   Reach out to someone else.
They say the best way to learn on a deeper level is to teach what you know. If you recall Zuri's story, it will interest you to know that I gained a lot from her when she came back and said she had used my principles.

If you want all of these lessons to become a part of your long-term strategy, you need to find someone who is also willing to embark on this journey – and teach that person all you know. While sharing your ideas, you will also learn a thing or two.

Some people want to get involved with real estate one day and start making a lot of money the following day. This book is going to empower you to think differently. You can achieve all you desire; but first, there are things you must put in place to ensure that you are on the right path to success.

Follow the steps you've got above carefully, plan, and execute; you will be amazed at how far you go with your real estate investment. With real estate, some people think it is just about buying and selling houses. There are numerous ways through which you can generate wealth - and we are going to discover them in the next chapter.

Thank you and I hope you enjoy this audiobook, the only thing is I ask is if you could please leave a review after listening.

Chapter Three

Numerous Ways to Build Wealth

There are one thousand and one different ways to build wealth, but when it comes to real estate, there are multiple distinct options. Real estate is not just buying and selling, as much as it is about having sustainable wealth through different avenues. This chapter will take you through all the numerous ways to build your wealth in real estate.

Generating wealth in real estate focuses on pooling all available resources and tapping opportunities to create the lasting wealth you desire. It is about knowing what works, applying it with the right timing, and having the patience to reap the benefits.

There are numerous, easy-to-follow, practical, and proven ways to build your wealth in real estate; but most importantly, you must ensure you have the determination, perseverance, and patience to pull it off. These three qualities are what distinguish the successful real estate investors from their less successful counterparts.

Zuri didn't only achieve her twelve property feat through these avenues, but with determination, perseverance and patience. You also can do the same and much more. Let's see the numerous ways to build your wealth in real estate.

1. Below Market Value Purchase

Buying and selling in real estate are only profitable when you buy at a low market price and sell at a high market price. It is the best way to maximise your profits. Certain conditions warrant the sales of a property below its market value. These conditions are the opportunities you must tap into as a real estate investor.

Some people who want to sell fast without hassle, lenders with foreclosures (REOs), and those that are misinformed about the market trends give rise to these opportunities. It is, however, vital to get your facts straight and not fall victim to investment frauds. Having the right, timely information can earn you a secured real estate investment below the market value.

This is a guarantee of generating lasting wealth.

2. The 'Appreciation' Effect

If you have been in existence for almost 3-4 decades, look around you; you can testify that things and times have changed. It is a known fact that in 5-10 years, there are changes in population, jobs, incomes, wealth, restrictions on development, immigration rates, construction costs, investors, and so on. These changes are on the high side known as the 'Appreciation' effect.

As a real estate investor, you should know that real estate properties tend to appreciate; the same goes for the factors that affect it. There will be population, jobs, income, and wealth increases as time goes by. And real estate properties will continue to appreciate. It means you can leverage on this fact to generate your wealth in real estate.

3. The Cash Flow System
In real estate, there is a belief that the primary source of cash flow is the rent - and it is true! The cash flow system allows you to use different factors to influence your cash flow. Inflation and an increase in market demand are such factors that can help boost your cash flows.

During inflation, interest rates are up, and you can generate more cash flow. As we progress further, we shall look at how you can manage your cash flow to help you create more wealth, so do read on.

4. Paying Off Your Mortgage through Amortisation
Investing in a mortgage is a secure avenue in real estate; the only tricky part is that while the property is in your name, its original owner can choose to retrieve it unless you pay it off. Amortisation is the process of paying off your mortgage with the rent collected on it. This is a means of generating more wealth.

Let's say you invest $10,000 in a mortgage worth $100,000; you pay it off with its rent after 20 years, you would have succeeded in acquiring a property worth ten times your investment and a 12 percent annual rate on the compound interest. This is pretty much a secured and guaranteed money-making venture in real estate.

5. Marketing for Profitability

What makes the difference in the business of real estate are the strategies and proper planning aimed at creating more profits after studying trends. A successful real estate investor is always on the lookout for positive trends in the market, new marketing strategies, and all it takes to generate more profits.

To achieve your goals of investing in real estate, you must be an effective marketer. Learn new strategies and study trends to generate more wealth.

6. The Value-Added Investment (VAI)

Have you ever seen a property that left you astonished and your jaws hitting the floor? There are many properties out there that are very different from their original architectural structures. As a real estate investor, calling more crowd would mean adding more value.

You can make cosmetic changes to your property, renovate it entirely, or give it the 'extra' features to increase your chances of attracting high-value customers. If you have a townhouse – turned - campsite, you can add a beautiful backyard to attract more customers.

We shall discuss how to increase the value of your property in a later chapter.

7. Maximising Inflation

Inflation is the decrease in the value of money due to the increase in the quantity of money in circulation. You may be wondering how inflation helps to generate more wealth in real estate. Here is how it works. When there is an increase in the amount of money in circulation, there is a price jump for properties, and rent increases - as well as interest rates.

You can maximise inflation by renting out your properties or selling them to the highest bidder at that time. You get to acquire more money during that period.

8. Enhancing the Neighbourhood

There are many popular neighbourhoods out there, and many real estate investors would love to invest there. Here is a secret for you; there are also many downtrodden and abandoned neighbourhoods that have the potential of being famous. Take your investment there, purchase at a low price, and sell when popular demand calls.

You also get to do the community a service by bringing development and civilisation to such neighbourhoods, which is a win-win situation for you.

9. Trending Conversions

An interesting fact about real estate is that it is a flexible field. It isn't limited to only one facet, and this gives it an advantage over other businesses. Conversions of properties based on trends and demand serve as a means of generating more wealth. A property can be converted into another based on its purpose.

If you have a property in a residential area which is fast becoming an industrial city, converting the apartment or home into an office building is a great way to generate more wealth. It is, however, important to study the trends and market demands before dabbling into such conversions.

10. Protection from Tax

You cannot build wealth when the government is swallowing your profits in the form of taxes. This is the reason you must put on the armour of protection to save your earnings. There are four ways to protect your profits from tax, and they are:

- **Depreciation:** This is the non-cash tax deduction on your properties. It is the tax paid on the remaining part of your property's net worth not generating income. It helps you minimise taxes paid.
- **Serial Home Selling:** This is another means of protecting your properties from tax. If you have a property in which you have resided for two years out of five, you can sell such property without paying tax. You can also keep reselling

such properties every two years and not spend a single dime on tax.

- **Retirement Plans:** There are tax-favoured retirement plans you can invest in and use all proceeds to invest in your real estate business.
- **Section 1031:** Section 1031 of the internal revenue code permits you to sell a personal property tax-free in exchange for purchasing a new one within a stipulated time.

Other ways of building wealth in real estate include realty stocks, discounted notes, tax liens, tax deeds, and many more.

The above methods of building wealth in real estate are mainly discussed to assure you enjoy sustainable wealth in real estate. Once you have the money to start investing, the outcome is predictable with adequate planning. This brings us to raising money for investing in real estate. The next chapter goes into details on raising the money needed for your real estate investments. Do read and enjoy.

Chapter Four

Raising Money

Having read up to this point, you will agree with me that we are getting there in regards to being educated and enlightened about real estate investments. This chapter is crucial as it teaches you how to raise money as a beginner in the real estate business. Read and learn more.

As popular as the demand for real estate investments is, having the money to invest - as well as the means of getting such money - is what matters. Real estate, unlike other businesses, requires a substantial amount of money to achieve success.

There are numerous means of raising money for real estate investments, but this chapter focuses on practical methods for beginners like you.

To make your money count, you must have the mindset of a farmer who cultivates rubber plants. The farmer knows that it will take him approximately six years to harvest the latex of the rubber plant, but remains undaunted and patiently waits while he does all necessary activities needed to produce his rubber tree and latex.

You must have the mindset that the money raised is the seed needed to yield the tree of sustainable wealth in real estate - and you must take all necessary measures to attain it.

The following are means of raising money for your real estate investments as a beginner:

1. Personal Funding

For anyone beginning the journey to financial freedom through real estate, this is the number one source of raising money for your investments. Personal funding refers to funding from your own pocket, using your savings, bonds, equity, mutual funds, and all other liquid assets. Personal funding saves you hassles from financial bodies, private investors, and other external contributors.

If you are good at sourcing for personal funds or you have family members and friends that can give you free money to start your real estate business, then you are good to go. This must, however, be done after setting goals and enumerating ways of achieving them.

Another method of personal funding is leasing your home out to start up and finance your real estate business. It is your home, and you can use the rent payments collected in refinancing your real estate business.

If you recall Zuri, my friend who got to follow all the principles in this book and ended up with a twelve property feat after five years, then let me tell you that Zuri started by leasing out all of the top floor rooms in her townhome. She converted her parents' room, the guest room, and the film room hall into a two bedroom apartment and leased it out as her first real estate investment.

You can start yours as Zuri did - or by buying a property with your funds to begin your real estate investment.

2. Other People's Funds

As a beginner, if you are short on cash or do not have any liquid assets to start your real estate investments with, here is an alternative - using other people's funds. This method of raising money may not be as easy as having your own funds; nevertheless, it doesn't seem all too bad. To achieve this feat, you must pay extra attention and learn the ropes of raising money from others.

No one would gladly invest in something without a certain percentage of guarantee that it would be successful. As a beginner, you must have SMART real estate investment goals that would convince the investors of their choice.

Having SMART investment goals is good, but most importantly, you must display a good sense of responsibility and be up front in your dealings. You may have people of good character validate that you have all it takes to invest wisely.

Other people's funds may include funds from private investors, creditors in the real estate business, private lenders, credit unions, bank loans, and so on. You can also be a middleman in the chain of distribution and use the money earned in refinancing your real estate investments.

You can engage in mortgage loans as well, and this is highly profitable as you can pay off the loan with the rent collected from the mortgage (amortisation, discussed earlier). Partnering with another trusted real estate beginner like yourself is also a great way of raising money for your real estate investments.

Of all of the above, a private investor is the best option as there are fewer protocols and requirements and more of friendliness, trust, and passion for succeeding to help make your real estate investments worthwhile.

3. Seller Funds

If you want to explore another facet of real estate known as Real Estate Wholesaling, this type of fundraising is what you should focus on as a beginner. Real estate wholesaling involves the scouting of potential and high-value buyers for sellers with properties and closing the deal. It is a middleman job and can help you raise money to finance your real estate investments.

With real estate wholesaling, you are preparing yourself to handle your own real estate investments while being exposed to the market trends and demands. This aspect of real estate requires negotiating and excellent communication skills. You must also be willing to sacrifice a lot of time and work twice as hard to please the seller.

This is how it works - you find a seller willing to sell fast and without corporate hassle, negotiate, and put into writing how you want him or her to fund the back work in getting a high-value buyer. Ensure any agreement made is documented and legalised to avoid future complications.

Then, you proceed to find interested and high-value buyers, give them a tour of the property, convince them to buy if it's a good deal for both sides, then close the deal. Make your own money and finance your real estate business. Easy, right? Just ensure you have adequate knowledge and avoid real estate investments scams.

Raising money for your real estate investments isn't as hard as it seems; it only requires your determination, perseverance, and patience to make it work. With the money raised through any of the above means, you can now proceed to invest in your real estate business. The next chapter will discuss how to handle your real estate business. Watch out for practical guides and tips.

Chapter 5

Real Estate is a Business - Handle it That Way

A real estate business is not different from an 8-4 job. A banker with a dream of being the Chairman of the Board of a big financial institution will start from scratch and work his/her way to the top. They would work hard, attend conferences, be on their best behaviour, and seek out promotions - all in a bid to achieve that dream. All other things being equal, with enough hard work, determination, and consistency, such a goal would come to pass.

A business should be treated more or less in the same way. Every successful business owner can attest to the fact that they had to manage the business as a priority and sacrifice a lot to achieve their dreams. Real estate is a business; hence, it must be handled as such. This chapter will educate you, as a beginner, on how to handle your real estate investments like a business.

Many real estate investors often see the real estate field as another side money-making venture; this has helped to distinguish the successful ones from others.

Real estate investments are not different from other businesses out there, and to become successful at it, you must be able to handle it as such.

These practical guides and tips for handling your real estate investments as a business are genuine and have been tested to yield quality results. These guides and tips were borne out of experience and lessons learned along the way of real estate investments.

It is essential you read and digest this chapter well, as this will take you to your desired goal of sustainable wealth through real estate.

Practical guides and tips on how to handle your real estate investments as a business:

1. Invest your full time.

As said earlier, many real estate investors often go into it with a mindset of a part-time venture. This has, however, not yielded the desired results. Since business isn't different from a day job – and real estate is a business - you should invest your full time in it. Full-time investments will enable you to focus and achieve optimal sustainability.

As a full-time real estate investor, you get to work with flexibility and achieve great results. You can answer calls at any time, get inspiration and ideas at any time, and make crucial decisions any time. You also get to learn a lot due to your full commitment and don't end up as a "Jack of all trades." Investing full time will allow you to pursue your real estate investment goals relentlessly.

Tip: If you can't invest your full time due to your job as you are depending on its stable income - or for any other reasons, do invest part-time. This only means you have to work twice as hard, be diligent and goal-oriented, multitask, and have a support structure.

The support structure could be your winning team (will be discussed later as one of the guides in handling your real estate business), your friends, or other reliable real estate investors you know. If you are into real estate business as a retirement plan, you must also invest quality time to achieve your goals. Real estate is a long term business, and it is like sowing a rubber seed to yield a rubber tree after many efforts and much time.

2. Set goals and plan ahead

There are no two ways about it; you must set goals and plan ahead. A business only thrives when specific goals are set and proper planning is ensured to meet the set goals. Everyone talks about setting goals, but how many do? As a beginner in real estate, you must avoid being like such people and set realistic goals.

Why should you set goals and plan for your real estate business? You must be able to define your purpose to achieve your desires. The setting of goals will require prioritising your needs and wants. It will also allow you to highlight the means of achieving them. This process will point out measurable milestones and ways forward.

There are short term and long term goals in real estate. Short term goals, as the name implies, refer to goals that are set to be achieved within a short amount of time. These short term goals also serve as milestones for long term goals. Examples of short term goals include leasing out part or all of your home, finding buyers for a property within some months, owning a property from a year's rent, and so on. These goals are achievable within their stipulated time frame.

Long term goals are goals set to be achieved in a long while. These goals are what you aim to accomplish over time with your real estate business. Long term goals are goals to be achieved in three to five years time. Examples include owning up to 10 properties in five years, being able to sustain yourself and your family with your business, setting up a real estate consulting firm, and so on. Long term goals may take time to be achieved, but through persistence, hard work, and determination, you can make it.

How to Set SMART Real Estate Goals

- **Define your goals regarding needs and time:** Your goals have to be specific and time-bound; hence, you have to define them regarding needs and time. For instance, Zuri's short term goal was to own a rental home after a year of leasing out a part of her townhome. This is an example of defining your goals regarding your needs and time. You may want something similar or something slightly different. Ensure they are realistic and achievable. Do not go overboard.

- **Prioritize your goals in order of importance:** What makes your goals SMART is the order of importance attached to them. In as much as you are working toward sustainable wealth through real estate business, your goals must be arranged in order of what is most important.

- **Analyse your goals for actualization:** This is a critical step in setting goals. You must analyse your defined goals to ensure that you can actualize them. Your goals must be realistic and achievable. You should set your goals based on your actual and potential resources. You should also look at your level of availability and commitment. Don't forget to factor external factors like economic situation, rules and laws, and other people that would be involved.

- **Evaluate often:** Now this may sound futuristic, but that's what it is. As you progress in your real estate business, ensure you make evaluations as you achieve your set goals. This allows you to set further goals or redefine your already set goals, depending on the progress status. This brings you to planning ahead of time and salvaging distressful situations.

Planning allows you to foresee any future losses as well as setbacks. Proper planning ensures adequate success in all your endeavors. It goes without saying that you must set goals and plan toward achieving them to succeed in your real estate business.

Tip: Since this is the jet age, you can make use of computer software to organise your goals, plans, and achievements. GoldMine, Microsoft Outlook, and ACT are examples of software programs you can employ.

3. Have the right attitude toward work.

For your real estate business to thrive, you need to have the right attitude toward work. Treat your real estate business the same way you would treat any other business - or rather how you would go about your office career. Attitude is everything; the right attitude toward work can help you land great deals, and can make the right impression on an investor. You must ensure you are at your best at all times.

Attitude to Portray in the Real Estate Business:

- **Be punctual:** Time is an essential factor in being successful. Many significant deals and connections have been lost as a result of not keeping to time. As a beginner in the real estate business, you must ensure you keep to time. When you schedule a meeting with your client, ensure you get there at least five minutes beforehand. You should also call ahead when you can't meet up with deadlines. This shows professionalism and discipline.
- **Be diligent:** Hard work plus consistency equals diligence. As a beginner in the real estate business, you can't afford to be less than diligent in your activities. Follow your plans accordingly, gather necessary information, be consistent, and strive to do your best. Diligence is the key to a successful business.
- **Dress appropriately:** As almost insignificant as this may seem, it is imperative. Your looks define who you are, so if you are aspiring to be a CEO, dress the part.
- **Pay attention to details:** Paying attention to details is a great trait you can develop with

conscious effort. This attitude is necessary in the real estate business. Being observant to all things can help you from falling into investments scams and frauds.

Tip: You should also be friendly and approachable as a beginner - but don't let your guard down. Everyone should see you as their go-to real estate investor, but you shouldn't be taken for granted. Note that it is crucial you separate business from pleasure to ensure professionalism.

4. Put together your winning team.

You are a winner; and your team is a vital part of ensuring your success in the real estate business. As a beginner, it is imperative you put together a team of competent and reliable people that can assure you of a smooth sail through your real estate business. These professionals must be experienced in their respective fields and be available to be of help when needed.

Your winning team should include:

- **A good real estate attorney:** You must hire or consult not any real estate attorney - but a good one. You need an attorney with enough knowledge about real estate to advise you about the risks and help you secure a great deal. He or she must also be able to suggest other practical transaction alternatives and be frank with you about your investments. Having a good attorney that can charge a reasonable fee is also an advantage.

- **A competent title company:** A title company is in charge of closing deals. To ensure a smooth closing, consult a qualified title company. Find a small and reliable company that caters to investors. Look into recommendations from trusted and successful real estate investors.
- **An experienced tax advisor:** One of the advantages of investing in real estate is having it easy when it comes to taxes. A qualified tax advisor will give practical advice on how to cut taxes and acquire as little as possible. An experienced tax advisor will also help in preparing the tax to pay from your business. Ensure you have adequate knowledge on whom to hire.
- **A handy contractor:** if you are trying to invest in 'conversions' or other rehabilitative types of real estate business, you need a helpful contractor. You need someone that is readily available to fix things within your proposed budget. A handy contractor must also be knowledgeable about trends and have the capacity to turn scraps into wonders. Hire a helpful contractor you can trust.

- **A mortgage broker:** Consulting a mortgage broker is necessary when investing in mortgages. It is essential you do your homework correctly before entrusting a mortgage broker with your business. Ask questions about those that have benefitted from their services. Ask for references and qualifications to prove competence and reliability.
- **A mentor:** As a beginner, it is vital you have someone that mentors you in the real estate business. You need a knowledgeable, reliable, and trustworthy mentor to guide through building your real estate business. You must also understand that this person has their own life to live, so tread with caution.

Tip: You can go into partnership in your real estate venture. Be an active partner and contribute adequately. You should also respect your partner's opinions and contributions. Learn diplomacy skills to enable you to make joint decisions.

5. Procure all necessary tools to the trade.

A business needs the right tools to function. You must gather information on the required tools needed to operate your real estate business smoothly. The tools required depend on the aspects of real estate you are considering. This book will discuss the essential tools needed as a beginner in the real estate business.

Essential tools to procure for your real estate business are:

- **An office with office essentials:** An office is vital for transactions and planning for your business. You can keep financial documents and hold crucial meetings or conference calls there. Necessary office essentials like a printer, photocopier, stapler, fax machine, a landline, printing paper, computer, and so on should also be procured. You can rent an office or use a room in your home as one.
- **Business cards:** These are essential to promote your real estate business. As a beginner, you may not be able to afford to make corporate cards; color business cards are affordable. You need to grow your connections; hence, your business cards must be professional and tell your story. Include the necessary information and you can even make them two-sided.
- **A website:** This is also important to reach out to your virtual clients and propagate your business to the world. If you are skilled in web development, then you can do it yourself. If you are not, you can seek the service of a freelance web developer on freelancing sites like Fiverr, Freelancer, and so on, at a very affordable price.

- **A Retrieval system:** There are times you are just not available and vital messages may come in. To avoid regrets for missing out on those messages, it is advisable that you purchase an answering machine. This will enable you to record the messages you have missed and then act on them.

Tip: Other tools you can indulge in are social media platforms, a business mail, wireless phone, and a PC or laptop. It is crucial you don't overdo it; don't forget you have to manage your cash flow.

6. Increase efficiency through recruitment.

As time goes on and your business progresses positively, you may need to recruit office staff. These staff members can include a receptionist, a secretary, and/or an assistant that will help to take some work off your shoulders. Hiring competent and trusted individuals is vital.

You can recruit people recommended by trusted individuals or search for your own. Do background checks to ensure you don't hire a criminal. You may not have the budget to hire extra hands, but you can employ multitaskers and people that are willing to see your business through to greater heights.

Hire people that can key into your business dreams and won't treat your business lightly.

Tip: You can hire one person to do all office work. That is, such a person will be the receptionist/secretary. You can also recruit another person to assist you in your field work and deal scouting; this person may serve as your right-hand man or woman.

7. Know the rules and abide by them.

Rules and laws are essential, and as a law-abiding citizen, you must ensure you identify these rules and abide by them. In real estate, knowing the rules is essential to close deals properly, make a proper foreclosure, record your transactions well, and create good contracts. Laws vary depending on location and jurisdiction; hence, you must know the local rules of where you want to invest.

You also need rules in the form of tenancy agreements to lease out your properties without consequences. As a beginner, don't be ignorant; ask questions so you don't get into trouble for what could be avoided. Below is a list of rules you need to know about in the real estate business.

- **Tenancy rules:** If you are aspiring to own properties you will lease out, then you need to have in-depth knowledge about tenancy. You must learn about the laws that bind you as a landlord with your tenants in that area. You should also know the clauses surrounding evictions, security deposits, and rentals. Visit the housing office in the secretariat located in that area for more information.

- **Inspections:** This is a critical step in buying or selling a property. Traditionally, an inspection is done after the property is under a contract. This gives an opportunity to those wanting to cut out of the deal using the excuse of finding a reason during inspection to do so. As a seller, you can ask for an inspection before drafting a contract to avoid unnecessary delays.
- **Recording rules:** For every transaction affecting your real estate business, you must make a record at the county office. You must learn the laws surrounding recordings such as the fees, deed, transfer tax, document sizes, and the legalizing of such recording. These rules differ from county to county within a particular state.
- **Choosing a closing agent:** While it is believed that it is the seller who gets to choose the title company for closing a deal, the buyer gets the chance as well. You can request a closing agent of your choice as a buyer.
- **Foreclosure deals:** It is in your best interest to learn about the rules guiding a foreclosure deal. There are technical details you need to know about a foreclosure deal before you can

trade in it. Ensure you have the right knowledge about it to avoid your transaction being nullified. Foreclosure rules differ from state to state, so take note of that.

- **Contract rules:** To ensure an official contract is drafted, you must learn the rules guiding it. Always insist on a formal draft to avoid legal issues. It isn't compulsory, but it helps you avoid legal problems.

Tip: Create a rapport with the locals where you want to invest, and ask them for help regarding those rules and how you can invest better. You can also log into the official website of the state to learn more about the rules or contact them to make enquires.

8. Secure great deals.

As important as bringing in money is to your real estate business, securing great deals is more important. As a beginner in the real estate business, the euphoria of bringing in more cash is always there. However, it is better when you can secure critical and significant deals that will open up constant cash flow for your business.

Spend your time and money on marketing and scouting for lucrative deals. You can even partner with investors to secure those deals if you are low on cash.

That one property you let go of to secure more deals will pave the way in acquiring more properties.

Tip: Learn about your weaknesses and strengths in managing a business. This will open your eyes to how to secure better deals. Leverage your strengths and work on your weaknesses to secure great deals for your real estate business.

As you can deduce from the above, real estate is a business and must be handled as such. The guides are practical and easy to follow. The tips are the unique secrets you would need to guarantee your success as a real estate investor.

Real estate business must be practiced defensively. The next chapter will discuss what defensive investing is all about and the principles guiding it. Do read and learn more.

Thank you and I hope you enjoy this audiobook, the only thing is I ask is if you could please leave a review after listening.

Chapter Six

Principles of Defensive Investing

In the previous chapter, you learned how to handle your real estate investments as a business, things to avoid, and tips to help you build your business. This chapter will focus on your real estate business as a defensive investment and the principles of defensive investing. You will learn what it means to invest defensively - be prepared to learn essential concepts here.

Defensive investing is the act of putting in money, hard work, and effort, gathering information and data, and managing your cash flows safely and securely to limit losses and avoid business setbacks. It is an indisputable fact that as an investor, you would prefer to create more wealth with the least risk through your real estate business.

Defensive investing allows you to focus on ways to limit your losses by avoiding investment scams and frauds, being part of unprofitable or shady deals, and investing at the wrong time. All these are what real estate investors take into consideration before venturing into the real estate world. If you are ready to invest defensively, ask yourself the following questions:

Am I prepared to create sustainable wealth through real estate?

Can I do all it takes to ensure I meet my set goals in achieving sustainable wealth?

Will I be able to stick it through until the end?

Once you can answer these questions, then you can proceed to learn about the principles that will guide you to invest defensively and create sustainable wealth through real estate. The following are the ten principles of defensive investing:

1. Have a long-term mind-set.
If you recall the second chapter of this book, which talked about avoiding the 'get-rich-quick' approach, this principle is very similar to that. Having a long-term mindset is necessary to invest defensively. You should have it at the back of your mind that you are sowing the seeds of a rubber tree or trying a weight loss plan.

You should note that both processes take a long while to see the results. Hence, you must be patient and focused to gain your desired results. Invest with the mindset of getting the dividends in the long run. You must nurture and train yourself to expect long-term effects. Avoid the 'get-rich-quick' approach with sought after, practical ways to achieve your sustainable wealth goals.

2. Timely information is key.

They say knowledge is power, but having the right expertise at the right time is wealth. To create wealth through real estate, you must always seek the correct information at the right time. It is crucial you have the right information - which is possessed at the right time - to secure a deal, to avoid losses and investment scams, and to own the right property at the right time.

Read books, seek advice, take courses, watch videos, and so on while engaging in a real estate business. This book is an excellent piece of information you have in your possession. Is it the right time?

You must also be reachable so that significant deals don't pass you by. Learn about the trends and markets. Be attentive and observant to notice changes that may affect your business.

3. Know your numbers.

As a real estate investor, you must know your real estate numbers to buy and sell correctly. There are seasons in the real estate business - and knowing them will help you know when to deal and when not to deal.

When market prices become low, you should know that buying will favor you at this point. You should also know when demands are high and the costs of properties are high.

Investing in a defensive manner means you must know all your numbers to maximize your gains and minimize your losses.

4. Buy, after calculating your profit.

Many times, losses are incurred after purchasing a property without digging into the profitability. As a beginner in the real estate business, always calculate your benefits first before buying any property.

You may be asking asking how you would know the profit on a long-term investment; it is simple. Be it a rental, a mortgage, or a property, it must fall into one of these to secure such deals:

- You can purchase it at a lesser price than its current market price.
- It can be converted and made into something better and much more valuable than its present state.
- It will provide sustainable income above its buying price.
- It will appreciate in a future market.

If your deal falls within any of those four categories, then be assured that you have a profitable deal; so act on it. A good deal can also vary from place to place, so ensure you have your facts straight to invest defensively.

5. Being 'safe' is paramount.

Being defensive in dealing means being safe in your investments. As a beginner, you should know that not all deals are secured and will lead to creating sustainable wealth. Some contracts have too high of a risk, and at the end of the day, may drive to huge losses. As a defensive investor, you must avoid that at all costs.

Learn what a good deal is; which is buying at a low price and selling at a high rate with enough profit to generate sustainable wealth.

A safe deal is a good deal with extra caution on things diving off to a wrong destination. This means regardless of how good the deal is, if it would cost you more to maintain than its proposed profits, then it isn't going to work.

For instance, fixer-uppers are known to be good deals, but for you as a beginner, you have to investigate to be sure such a deal isn't a waste of time. You need to seek the service of a professional to evaluate the property and notify you of its worth before dealing. You must ensure that any rehabilitative work done to fix the property won't consume too much of or waste your time and money.

Defensive investing involves being safe at all times. Even when there are risks to take, ensure the chances are low enough to be combatted as a beginner.

6. Manage your cash flows.

Every successful real estate investor refers to their cash flow; this shows how important the term is in the business of real estate. It is essential you understand how to operate and manage your cash flow as a defensive strategy of investing.

Having the right information on how to manage your cash flow is essential. How to determine the cash flowing for you in your real estate business is also vital to the success of your business.

As a beginner, it is advisable to have more cash reserves to avoid lending from banks or financial bodies. It is also advisable you keep cash with you and coming in, rather than pouring it all on some property. Several unforeseen matters arise unexpectedly; your cash flow can take care of such issues and still run your business smoothly. Hence, manage it wisely!

7. Know ways to exit.

Being defensive involves conscious effort to invest in safe deals and incur minimal losses. There are times when, despite all caution, things don't turn out as expected. When such results are discovered early, it is best to use an exit strategy to salvage the situation.

Exiting from a deal may occur as a result of blind deals with no profits or potential losses. It is vital to learn the ways to exit such agreements. Several exit options exist depending on the situation.

A chapter in this book will discuss in details the various options of exit strategies available. This will enlighten you on how to salvage some risky situations.

8. Earning it is right, keeping it is important.

What makes the difference in your defensive investments is whether you can hold on to your acquired wealth without any issues. Many real estate investors do battle with lawsuits and other problems that may allow them to end up losing their property or going bankrupt.

It is crucial you learn how to keep your wealth. Avoid shady deals that may come back to haunt you. Learn to keep records of all your activities and transactions. It is safe to say that learning about the several real estate rules, and abiding by them, will also help you secure your wealth.

Get educated on other investors' legal mistakes and how taxes work to avoid trouble with the law and authority. Be sure to go through the right and proper process of buying a property, leasing out a property, selling a property, or making deals.

It is vital to insure all your properties so as to keep them safe and not incur as many losses during setbacks like disasters, fire outbreaks, and so on. Insurance is key - and it defends you as an investor. Don't acquire lots of liabilities as an investor; secure your properties with good insurance policies.

Setting up a corporation or LLC can also protect you from acquiring liabilities as an investor. As your business continues to expand and grow, it would be safer to set up a corporate entity that would protect them all.

Earn your wealth, but also learn to keep it well to avoid wasting all the effort you put into it. Don't say "I was not aware." The same way you acquired the wealth, you can quickly lose it. Secure your wealth through the above plans and more from what you've learned.

9. Don't fall for investment scams

This is another means of keeping your hard-earned wealth. Many people are out there looking for those to defraud; and if you aren't careful, you may fall victim. Several real estate investors are after fast deals; hence, they fall victim of enticing and appealing fake deals. They cry foul, not knowing they allowed themselves to be swayed by the sweet words and fraudulent deals of marketing frauds.

Some investment scams may look like the real deal, but don't fall for them. Gather enough information and facts so you can distinguish the authentic from the fake.

The following are the traditional investment scams out there:

- A deal with a requirement of little or no down payment.
- You are getting your cash back at closing.
- Wholesale deals with obviously inflated prices.
- Mortgage elimination scams.
- Syndication scams (will be discussed in a later chapter).

When faced with people involved in things like this, avoid them like the plague. Don't let them persuade you to invest poorly. Invest wisely and defensively.

10. This is your goal, make it count.

The last principle of defensive investing is to see it as a goal and to make it count. It is no different from seeing a real estate investment as a business and handling it as such. Treat your defensive investments like a goal; hence, make it count in cash and kind.

Define the purpose of your defensive investments, prioritize them in order of importance, analyse your options, and evaluate the outcomes. Know that you are aiming toward sustainable wealth creation; hence it is essential to give it your best.

Defensive investing is the way to succeed in your real estate business. Master the principles and all your dreams shall come true. The next chapter will discuss an important aspect of defensive investing, which is managing your cash flow. Your cash flow is of huge importance in a successful real estate business. Learn how to manage it in the next chapter.

Chapter seven

How to Manage your Cash Flow

In the real estate field, it is essential to have a detailed understanding of what cash flow is all about to enable you to manage it appropriately. Cash flow is the amount of money in circulation to run a particular business. It isn't enough to have just the start-up; it is also essential to have a consistent source of cash to run and flourish the business to your desired level.

Cash reserve is the constant money you have in the bank or at hand that you can spend from on building your business. Unlike cash flow, which is consistent as it comes from the money made from rent, selling of properties, or the extra cash from a mortgage, a cash reserve is a fixed price that keeps reducing as you spend it.

There are so many issues that arise in a real estate business, and as an investor, you must have the necessary resources to salvage the situation. Otherwise, you run into more problems and an ultimate financial disaster. It is essential to have a considerable amount in your cash reserve as a beginner in the real estate business.

The following four factors help to determine the amount to be budgeted into your cash reserve:

- **The rental market:** The lesser the rates of vacancies, the smaller the amount needed in your cash reserve. You will only need a little amount of money to make a vacancy ad in your local newspaper. Also, spend more time screening the tenants, their credit reports, and employment verification to prove that they would be able to pay the rent when due.
- **Cost and time of eviction:** There are times when the expense of evicting a tenant, especially through legal means, may determine the need for a cash reserve. The time frame of evicting a tenant and finding a new tenant may depend on the property, especially a mortgage. A cash reserve must be adequately provided to buffer the effect of that time frame.
- **The property's age:** This will affect your cash reserve as an older property may need repairs, fixing, or renovations - and this may cost a lot. The cost can only be covered by the amount in your cash reserve.
- **The neighbourhood:** Low-income neighbourhoods will lead to a need for more money in the cash reserve, while the opposite is true for high-income neighbourhoods. Neighbourhoods

with multi-unit buildings with smaller units will also lessen the amount needed in your cash reserve.

Cash flows and cash reserves are both essential to running a real estate business. When you run out of cash flows, you can rely on your cash reserve to save the day. When you are out of cash reserves, look inward to generate more cash flow.

Cash flows help you make rational business solutions due to the confidence that you have something to rely upon. It helps you to secure deals that need down payments. With enough cash flow and reserves, you can think calmly and make profitable decisions, which is impossible to make when cash-strapped.

You may decide to wait for a higher sales price of property before you start selling; only cash flows and cash reserves can grant you such luxury. It is important to plan for how to generate consistent cash flows and reserves.

Generating cash flows and cash reserves:

- You can create your cash reserves from a good-paying job, long-term investments, or family and friends.
- If you don't have a means for a cash reserve, you can partner with trusted real estate investors to close a deal. Ensure the partner is safe to deal

with - no scams involved. Draft a legal document regarding your benefits from such a partnership.

- Save money before investing in significant properties. This can be from your other sources of income or the sales of some belongings.
- Backup funds are essential in generating cash flows and reserves. These backup funds include credit cards and credit lines that can be employed during emergencies.
- Wholesale deals of fix-and-flips to generate cash can also build a cash reserve. If you can't buy the "fixer-upper" properties yourself, you can help the seller find suitable buyers and make money as a middleman. With this, you can employ the double-closing method to buy and flip properties without using your funds. You get to close the second deal from the profit made from the first closing.
- Sometimes your title company may not approve double-closing; an alternative is the contract assignment. The contract assignment is one in which the buyer/seller assigns a purchase contract to another real estate investor to close in their place. Only one closing occurs in a contract assignment - no issues generated.

Cash flows and reserves can be managed by using facts and figures. Invest more to generate more cash flows, make partners secure deals, or source for other means of income. Ensure you spend the money wisely on things that matter and don't overspend. As a beginner in real estate, consult your mentor, browse the internet, or reach out to successful real estate investors to learn more about managing your cash flows effectively.

You must also be vast in closing deals - and you need money to close deals. The next chapter will enlighten you on how to get your closing money. Read and enjoy.

Chapter Eight

Getting 'Closing' Money

Acquiring investments in real estate is very easy with all you have learned from the previous chapters; the critical thing to learn now is how to close deals. Closing off deals requires money the majority of the time. While real estate business requires huge capital and other means of sourcing for funds, the funds needed to close your deals can be outsourced from other methods or gotten through some other transactions. This chapter will enlighten you about the various means of getting the closing money for your real estate business.

These means have been tested and verified to be authentic. If you can still recall my friend Zuri who acquired twelve properties in five years, I am pleased to tell you that Zuri practiced all that was taught in this chapter and was able to source for her closing money with ease. I remember how she kept beaming with smiles after closing her first deal from the money saved up from the rent payments from her townhouse.

There are several means of getting your closing money; study them well and practice whichever suits your situation and financial status.

The following are ways to get your closing money:

Personal savings: If you have up to five figures or more in savings, you can close your deals with your own money. These savings could be from other ventures, a trust fund, or a well-paying job. Personal savings are the best option for cash needed to close deals as there would be no hassle and no need to repay. You can also save up the profit made from the deal for future closings.

Selling off assets: This is another personal means of raising closing money. You may be someone with lots of acquired assets which are no more in use. For instance, cars, boats, expensive furniture, sports gear, and more may be sold at reasonable prices, thus generating the income required to close your deals. If these assets are ones you can't bear to part with, but are not in use, then see it as a temporary parting to gain more in the future.

Cash from your home or rental's equity: Equity from your home is the money earned from renting it out after years of you living there. This was how Zuri started her real estate business. The money earned from a year's rent was used to close her first deal of a rental home. If your home is quite big and you can maximize it as a rental to give you more profits, you can consider downsizing. Moving into a smaller apartment is known as downsizing.

The substantial capital your house is generating can be used to invest in your real estate business. Don't miss out on the opportunity to create more sustainable wealth.

Bring in partners: If you have some cash, but can't meet up with the whole cost needed to close the deal, you can bring in partners. You can leverage on the money from others to close your sales; ensure they are people you trust and have legal backing for all transactions made.

Borrow money from money-lenders and financial institutions: Lending money from private investors and financial institutions can help you source for large amounts of money for large deals. The only issue there is that there are lots of hassles and protocols to deal with. You must also have collateral to borrow colossal amounts of money.

Down payment assistance from governments: There are individual cities and states in the US like Oakland, California, Chicago, Miami, Houston, and so on whose non-profit organizations providing down payments for citizens who haven't owned a home during a certain number of years. For more information, seek information on the state's official website of head office.

There are several other means of getting your closing money which include; credit cards, student loans, borrowing from the real estate commission, selling a part of your property, prepaid rent, tenants' security deposits, lease-options, and so on.

Getting your closing money isn't that hard; through persistence and determination, you can do it. Ensure you don't fall into investment scams and verify your options thoroughly. You can never be too careful, so seek for trusted friends' and allies' opinions and seek consultation from a professional. Beware of predatory lenders.

All of the options above can be employed depending on the type of deal needing to be closed and your financial status. Build wealth to achieve your business goals; closing significant deals will lead you to the financial freedom being propagated by the real estate business.

Now to move forward, we will be discussing how to increase the value of your property. Your property(s) is/are your prized possession(s). You must increase the value(s) of your property(s) to create more sustainable wealth.

You will learn certain things you can do to enhance the value of your property and attract high-income customers. Do read, digest the points, and learn from them.

Chapter Nine

How to Increase the Value of Your Property

Your property tells who you are, and that's why successful real estate investors have high-valued properties. As an aspiring landlord, it is imperative you think from the tenant's point of views as they hold the key to your sustainable wealth.

When you purchase a property for rentals, how to make it attractive for the high-income customers is what runs through your mind as a real estate investor. This implies that the value of your property lies with the type of clients that would make use of the property.

As a beginner in the real estate business, you should know that your clients should be valued to get the maximum profits from your transactions. Whatever conversions you hope to make or type of aspect you want to venture into in real estate, the kind of money you wish to generate all revolve around the CLIENT. Hence, it is crucial you value your esteemed clients to maximise profits.

This chapter is dedicated to teaching you how to increase the value of your property, by valuing your clients, to create sustainable wealth. When you value your customers, it invariably means you will do everything to satisfy their needs. The most important has to do with the property itself.

Like discussed earlier, your property is your prized possession. Hence, you must treat it as such. As a real estate investor, your ultimate goal is to create sustainable wealth; and this can only happen when you have high-valued properties that will attract high-income customers. These high-income clients will generate that sustainable wealth through high-paying and stable rents.

In monetary terms, the value of your property can be estimated as:

$$\text{Value(V)} = \text{Net Operating Income(NoI)} \div \text{Capitalization rate(R)}.$$

For instance, say you have a rental property that brings in a net operating income of $56,000 a year. After various consultations with experts in the real estate business, you figured the property could sell with a capitalisation rate of 8 per cent. With these two values, your property is valued at $700,000.'

$$56000(\text{NOI}) \div 0.08(\text{R}) = \$700,000(\text{V})$$

If, through some means, you were able to increase the NOI to $65,000, then you would have succeeded in increasing its value by 14 per cent. This means you would have a profit of $112500 as equity.

$$65,000(\text{NOI}) \div 0.08(\text{R}) = \$812500$$

Let's make it sound even better; you can reduce the risks attached to the property and consequently reduce the cap rate even further to about 7 per cent. With a higher NOI and a lower cap rate, you are bound to have a high-valued property.

$$65,000(\text{NOI}) \div 0.07(\text{R}) = \$928571(\text{V})$$

From a value of $700,000 to $928571, your property is high-valued. You would probably ask if this is even possible. Yes, it is very possible. As a landlord, with the aim of creating sustainable wealth, you can increase the value of your property by increasing its NOI through high-income customers. The capitalisation price can also be reduced by reducing the risks attached to the properties. All of these would add up to increase your property value.

How can you increase the value of your property? Here's how:

- Put together a new makeover for the interior.
- Ensure safety, security, and convenience at all times.
- Make the rooms the right size according to the function of each.
- Add more storage space.
- Identify what generates noise and try to eradicate or ameliorate it.
- Give your curb the most attractive look ever.
- Engage in services that are beneficial aside from rent collection.
- Make new great conversions from the garage, attic, or basement.
- Convert the property into something more in trend.
- Reduce operating costs to increase your cash flow.
- Old people are important, value them well.
- Improve the overall appearance of your property.
- Adhere to all zoning and building regulations.
- Go with a unique look no client can resist.
- Get rid of disturbances from your neighbours.
- Play a bit of politics.
- Apply market demand to determine rent rates.
- Effective communication with tenants is important.

- Allow your property to stand out amidst competition.
- Create an apartment checklist to ensure you achieve all your goals.

The above and much more are ways to increase the value of the property. You can come up with your own strategy depending on what you desire. Having high-paying clients can be achieved when your property is highly valued.

Chapter Ten

Winning through Negotiations

Finding significant deals is important, but winning them is what matters most. Several factors affect the closing of deals, but few factors make it successful. Negotiation is one of those few factors that can ensure your winning. Negotiating is the act of achieving a purpose through skillful and strategic discussions. Negotiating should be a calm process with no fights or spitting into each other's faces.

Negotiating is an act of discussing to reach an agreement; hence, you have to learn the language to speak, the subtle cues, and the body language involved. Negotiation isn't always a win-win, and as a beginner, the earlier you learn to face reality, the better. Negotiate with buyers, sellers, or clients to earn desired deals. With a more conciliating approach, you can convince anyone to give into what you want.

In the real estate field, many successful investors were able to negotiate their way into their desired deals. It isn't calculus or Greek, but the simple act of convincing the second party to give you what you want.

This chapter will discuss how to win deals through negotiation. It will highlight and explain how to negotiate to gain your desired deals. Winning significant and sizeable deals will help you attain sustainable wealth. Negotiating your way through such deals is essential. So, read on and enjoy.

How to win your deals through negotiating:

1. Know what you want.
This is the first step in the negotiating business. Identify your wants and needs from the deal. Put all of it into consideration while negotiating with the second party. To gain your desired deal, study your strengths and weaknesses in communicating and persuading people to give in. Learn to be charismatic during a negotiating session, dress the part, and sell your strengths.

Knowing yourself will help you negotiate better and secure the deal you are aiming to acquire.

2. Be informed about the property and the neighbourhood.
This is the second step to consider for negotiating that dream deal. As a beginner in the real estate business, it is imperative you have adequate knowledge and information about the property you aim to acquire. This isn't only to enhance negotiations, but to avoid

getting into investment scams. Knowing the neighbourhood is also an additional advantage.

Seek knowledge from the people living in the neighbourhood, the occupants of the property (if any), or the seller himself. With such experience, you have the power to negotiate better and make the most out of it. Do your homework properly to win that deal to desire.

3. Investigate the seller.
This sounds like an FBI mission, but it is crucial in your negotiations. Having vital information about the seller can give you the upper hand at the negotiation table. Run a background check, ask people that are familiar with the seller, ensure you know how they deal. Also seek information about similar deals the seller has carried out to have an insight about the kind of deal you are likely to have.

With this information about the seller, you can know if it's a quick deal or the seller is in search of the highest bidder. You can also ensure the deal is lawful and there are no scams involved. Tilt the deal to your side by having vital information about the seller which is necessary to influence your negotiations.

4. Identify favourable claims.
There are times when the seller brings up claims that are way too exaggerated to support their offer. Such

claims include add-ins, appraisals, and a past purchase price that has been exaggerated. It is in your best interest to identify those claims and subtly disprove or undermine them. You can also use the information to your advantage to convince the seller to accept your offer.

It is advisable to use a very subtle approach to avoid causing conflicts or confrontations from the seller. This is the essence of gathering information before going to the negotiating table. Create favourable claims of your own to increase the emotional appeal on your offer.

5. Deal to buy.

What makes some deals last just four or six weeks at most is the buyer's willingness and readiness to buy. Convince the seller that you are ready to buy once you can reach an agreement and a more severe negotiation would be tabled. Coming to the negotiation table prepared to purchase gives you an edge in negotiating your offer.

With all the necessary information about the property and its neighbourhood, the seller, the value, the financial implications, and economic status, you should be prepared to buy when offered a good deal. Explain this to the seller and convince them to accept your offer.

6. Put in more than you expect in your proposal.

When drafting your offer proposal, put in more than you are expecting. This is because many sellers like to beat down the price until they are assured they have more to gain. With a higher amount than you expect, you can get more, all, or almost all of your offer.

Negotiate based on this amount despite having your real offer in mind. Note that you are aiming to get the most you can from the deal.

7. Your credibility matters.

A good deal requires a lot of credibility on the sides of all parties involved. Negotiate the deal with your credible status. Convince the seller with your character, credit status, capacity, and consistency. With this, you can earn some brownie points from the seller and gain more from your offer. No one likes to deal with someone that is not of credible status.

This means you should portray yourself as a reliable, trustworthy, and competent buyer.

8. Negotiate for yourself.

When it comes to important or huge deals, it is advisable to negotiate them yourself. As a beginner in the real estate business, it is crucial you handle the delivery yourself. This is to ensure that things go well and your interests are adequately considered.

An agent is a no-no, so it's not an option.

9. Never offer the 'split the difference' way out
After a series of negotiations, should you discover that you are at a dead-end, many investors do go for the 'split the difference' way out. It means that the difference between the offers is split up and added to both sides. This means you get lower than you bargained. Even if this is the only way out, never be the first to suggest it.

If the seller suggests it, that's all well and good. You tend to lose more when you do. When the seller initiates it, you can leverage on it to place your offer on the table again and bargain higher.

10. Leave something on the negotiation table to finalise the deal.
Many negotiations do end with one party unhappy with the outcome. You can ensure that you get a lot out of the offer while making the seller feel like they did as well. Leaving a little money out from your proposal, may not be totally beneficial to you, but can earn you a smile from the seller.

Sacrifice a little to maintain cordiality as, who knows, you could need help from the same seller in the future.

Don't jeopardise the relationship just because you couldn't compromise a little.

Negotiating is a two-way approach and you must tread with caution so as not to cause conflicts. Have access to all necessary information to enable you to get the most from the deal. Utilise a subtle approach to disprove or undermine claims from the seller. Above all, with adequate negotiation, you can win your huge deals and generate sustainable wealth.

Chapter Eleven

How to Invest for Maximum Gain

Real estate investment has been proven to be an authentic investment that can guarantee sustainable wealth. You have learned how real estate can serve as a pathway to sustainable wealth. You also discovered the numerous ways to build wealth and how to raise money in real estate. How to handle your real estate investments as a business and the principles of defensive investing have been discussed, and you learned a lot as well.

Achieving sustainable wealth through real estate is all about making money and maximising your gains. This chapter focuses on how to invest for maximum gain. There are several branches of real estates to venture into, and each can bring you sustainable wealth. These aspects of real estate can be explored to maximise your gain. Read this chapter and learn more.

Investing for maximum gain focuses on how to expand your host of money-making ventures in real estate business. It involves discovering the several ways of making more money in your estate business. As earlier discussed, the business of real estate is beyond buying and selling. As a beginner in the real estate business, you must know the other means of investing in real estate to maximise your gain. This way, you have multiple income streams, and you get to achieve the desired real estate goals.

The following are the means of investing to maximise your gains:

1. Long-term residential rentals:
This is one of the traditional methods of investing in real estate business. Long-term residential rentals refer to the process of owning a rental property and renting it out to tenants. This is a great investment plan as it is consistent and stable. It helps to generate adequate cash flows needed to run your real estate business.

It is an undeniable fact that the population increases and there is always a demand for residences to accommodate the growth. This leads to people renting homes, or buying for those fortunate enough. There are always young adults who want to live alone and college students who want out of college dorms or on-campus residences.

People migrate from one town to another and need a place to stay either temporarily or permanently. All these put together implies that residential rentals are in high demand and a lucrative way of investing to maximise profits.

To make this investment worthwhile, ensure you own a great place that is attractive to your desired customers. Also, ensure it is in a great location to serve as an advantage. Ensure your tenancy contracts are beneficial for your desired clients.

Long-term residential rentals, if properly managed, can result in retirement investments. It can also be passed down from generation to generation - hence, serving as long-lasting wealth for your family.

2. Real estate ETFs and mutual funds:

A real estate exchange-traded fund (ETF), is a collection of stocks or bonds in a single fund. These funds are similar to index funds and mutual funds, due to the fact that they come with the same broad diversification and low costs overall.

These stocks come from real estate investments trusts (REITs) and are authentic. To maximise your gain, you can invest in this area with the profits you have made in order to earn more. It is safe once you get the hang of it.

Real estate mutual funds are another means of maximising profit and generating sustainable wealth. These funds have low costs and low track record, hence, can serve as a side attraction in optimising your gain.

3. Fix-and-flip investments:

This is another traditional means of real estate investment. This investment is very profitable as it allows you to maximise profit with small investments. Conversions of properties according to market trends and demands can also be looked into. It differs from residential rentals as these homes have to be converted from their original forms to something more enticing.

Learn the act of renovating homes with a low budget. You should use the principle of majoring on the inexpensive repairs and minoring on the expensive ones, for starters. Learn creative ways of doing renovations without much money. Consult experts in this field and make your investments count.

Fix-and-flip type of real estate investment is an advisable real estate investment for beginners in the real estate business. Ensure you verify the property you want to flip properly to avoid investment scams. Being creative is all it takes to make it big in this type of investment.

4. Short sales:

There are times that a real estate investor may be behind in the payment on their mortgage and need a way out. If the property is yet to be foreclosed, then a short sale may occur. All the parties involved in the mortgage possession must reach an agreement before such transactions occur. After the deal, the property is sold for a lesser price than what is left of the mortgage. This is a great chance to invest and buy below the market value.

This investment is lucrative, but also risky. You have to pay in cash, and it may not be safe to do so. It is, however, profitable as you get to inspect the property and know what you are getting into. Do a fair job of negotiating, and you could be leaving with an investment worth hundreds to thousands more than you invested.

With adequate patience and an eye for a good investment, you can pull it off and maximise your gain.

5. Real estate Investment Trusts (REITs):
For investments in real estate without owning physical property, real estate investment trusts are the key. They allow you to invest in properties without owning them physically. This aspect of real estate is new and has been discovered to be profitable for those that know how it works.

With REITs, you can achieve your real estate goals through diversifying. It is a long term investment - and as long as you know the market trends, you will be fine. Invest your profits in this and maximise your gains. Attain everlasting wealth with real estate investments trusts.

6. Vacation rentals:

Think about this - the massive influx of tourists in Miami, Los Angeles, and California translates into more wealth for you. Having vacation homes in places with tourist attractions can be a good strategy in maximising your gain. You can buy reasonable properties and turn them into vacation homes for tourists.

You can make a lot from this type of investment and save up a lot. It has been proven to be highly profitable and secure as an investment in real estate. Managing a vacation home isn't expensive. Hence, there are more ways to make money. List your property on the internet and create a website to attract more customers.

Another interesting fact about this type of investment is that you may not even own a single property to participate in it. All you need do is to set up connections and manage vacation homes to maximise your gain. Utilise the power of leverage to create profitable relationships to give you an edge. Come up with great strategies that would attract clients to the vacation homes you want to manage. Manage them well and earn great reviews for the promotion of your business.

7. Hard-money lending / private investing:

Hard money lending is short-term lending of loans to people without financial means to close their deals or invest in real estate. This method of investing is fast and has a huge interest rate. Many people are in desperate need of money to close significant and profitable deals. Identify such real estate investors and sweep in to save the day.

As a private investor, you are assured of getting your money back when due. Since your interest rate is also high, you get to generate a lot of income. To kick-start this business, ensure you have a significant amount of capital or partner with other reliable investors for this. You don't need huge money, just enough to start and you can keep refinancing with the profits made.

It will increase your cash flow and give you opportunities to save enough to invest in great deals as well. This is an authentic way of achieving sustainable wealth in the real estate business.

8. Commercial real estate

As a beginner in the real estate business, it is advisable to focus on a type of investment. As time goes on and you make progress, you can diversify and start looking into other income streams. Commercial real estate is the owning and managing of multiple units of properties ranging from residential homes to office buildings, to shopping malls, and so on. Diversification will boost your cash flows and help you attain sustainable wealth faster.

Many successful real estate investors today are into commercial real estate. It is profitable and long-term. It is the type of investment to pass from one generation to another. It is a great way to maximise your gain in real estate.

The above real estate investments are ways to maximise your gain in the real estate business. With the goal of everlasting wealth in real estate, you can't afford to put all your eggs in one basket. Spread your wings to generate more wealth and be successful in your real estate business. As a beginner, it won't be easy; but with hard work, persistence, and patience you will get there. If Zuri can own 12 properties in five years, nothing should stop you from achieving the same and much more.

All you need is to be visionary, ambitious, and ready to take action at all times. Your reading this book is a sign that you desire sustainable wealth and are a step closer to achieving it.

Chapter Twelve

Becoming a Successful Landlord

Congratulations in advance on owning your first rental property. Yes, you deserve the congratulations for becoming a potential landlord. If you understand everything that has been discussed in this book up to this point, then you deserve the compliment. You can proudly call yourself a real estate investor; all you need to do is to take actions.

Have you ever wondered how you will feel when you become a successful landlord? If you haven't, then start thinking about it. Owning a property is cool; and renting the property out and making cool cash from it is a step toward your real estate dreams. When you become a successful landlord, then you can say you have achieved your goals.

This chapter will focus on grooming you to become a successful landlord. You have learned how to increase the value of your property to attract high-income clients in a previous chapter. You will learn how to get those clients, how to make their stay memorable, and how to keep them. So, pick up your pen and learn more.

If all you dream of is becoming a successful landlord, then listen up, YOU CAN DO IT. The whole journey to get there may seem long and complicated; but really, after reading this book up to this point, you are halfway there. All you need is to put it all into actions and make your dreams come true.

Having a rental property and maintaining it with tenants is not an easy task. As a beginner in the real estate business, you have to decide if you want to call the shots yourself or recruit someone capable of doing that. Property management can be quite taxing and demanding; and it's not necessary you take on the role yourself.

Property management may be through hired management or self-management. Hired management leads to passive control of your property by delegating managerial activities to a caretaker or a property management company. This process allows you to have more time on your hands to do other activities, as well as providing professional management of your property.

A caretaker is someone hired with the knowledge and experience of property management. The caretaker looks into all the necessary details of property management you delegate. You may decide to give them almost full autonomy in handling your tenants and the property. You may also be involved in important decision making, policies, procedures, and all other significant issues concerning your property and tenants.

It is advisable to employ an older and more experienced person as a beginner, to reach a level of professionalism and avoid your property being managed by unfit hands. You may also give the job to a reliable tenant, whom you are giving all or almost all rent off as incentive. Whichever options you chose, ensure you recruit a trustworthy and competent person.

A property management company is one that specialises in managing multiple rental units of different property owners. This company is experienced and has competent professionals skilled in property management. It may be expensive and not specific in strategies, but when it comes to professionalism, it's the right choice.

Self-management is the act of managing your property by yourself. As a beginner in the real estate business, it is advisable you go into this, at least for your first property, and subsequently you can employ hired management. You may ask how it's possible with no experience or knowledge whatsoever. Here's the reply; it's possible, for you have this book to guide you right!

Self-management helps to save costs of hiring someone or a company. With self-management, you can learn first-hand the process of managing a property. You also get to be exposed to the world of property management and learn the ropes of how the market works. You are allowed to make mistakes, take risks, and move ahead, sure you are doing it right. Exercise patience, consult with other experienced real estate investors in this field, and read to learn more about it.

For adequate and excellent self-management, you must learn how to become a successful landlord. You will learn the ten principles of becoming a successful landlord.

1. Understand the buyer's risks.

It is an indisputable fact that buying a property comes with lots of risks. As a beginner, you have to ensure you avoid them by understanding what those risks are. When purchasing a property, be sure it is the one you truly want and you have the necessary means to acquire it. Inspect the property correctly and ask for a formal report on the status of the property. Consult a professional in property inspection to get your desired results.

Do a background check on the property by asking neighbours, occupants, and others that know about it.

Ask them how the property has been run in the past, how they perceive it, its advantages and disadvantages. Ask if there had been any issues, civil or criminal, attached to the property. Ask all the right questions to avoid falling into investments scams.

If the property is currently occupied by tenants, ask for tenant rent tolls and files. This will enable you to have an insight into the tenants occupying the property and their rent payment attitudes. Verify security deposits transferred from the seller to you. Confirm that it is authentic and have documentation to that effect.

Learn about the rules and laws binding the property in that area or vicinity. Ask for any permits, licenses, zoning, building regulations, and occupancy laws associated with the property. Ask carefully and ensure they are rules you can abide by.

Get copies of warranties and service contracts the tenants signed with the seller. Review them properly and ensure you are okay with them and can maintain them all. After purchasing the property, arrange for insurance coverage to minimise future losses. With all these things taken into consideration, you can be assured you are acquiring a property with little or no risks.

2. Have the property suitable for rentals.

If your rental property still has tenants from the previous owner, do well to honour the existing rental agreements. Comply with the rules and regulations and start looking into vacancies as soon as various tenants' contracts are coming to an end.

To prepare for vacancies, you have to think about the group of tenants you would like to accommodate. Your goal is sustainable wealth through real estate investment, so ensure that you target high-income clients or high-paying clients. Clients like college students, Senior families, young professionals, empty nesters, and so on are examples of high-paying clients.

To begin the process of making your property suitable for renting and to attract high-paying clients, clean and paint to give it a new look. Do thorough inspections to ensure every appliance is working. All broken locks, windows, doors and screens should be repaired or replaced. Make renovations if possible and install new fittings to make it suitable and attractive for renting.

It's not enough to have the place good-looking and attractive; adding value through tenant-friendly services is the total package. As the landlord, ensure you are friendly and approachable to create a good rapport with your tenants. Allow for some freedom and tenant autonomy by accepting pets, furniture and appliances.

Put in hot-button features to attract your desired clients. Hot-button features like great kitchens and bathrooms, amazing views, vast storage, nice parking lots, study areas, soundproof walls, open floor plans, and roommate-friendly plans can be included in your preparation.

Create friendly terms and conditions, and make security deposits and rent payments flexible by allowing for payments in instalments. Include tenant likes and dislikes when deciding on the rental rates. In essence, ensure your tenants are comfortable leaving and happy with the lease rules and regulations, terms and conditions, and physical features.

3. Attract high-paying residents.
To attract high-paying residents, you have to put up your vacancies in places with potential high-paying clients. Utilise the media and promote your vacancy ads to attract your desired customers. Put up ads in commercial areas, on campuses, and other places where your potential clients can be found. Put together a sales message that highlights the hot-button features of your property as well as benefits for the residents. Explain why your property is the best, and it should be chosen by your desired customers.

When potential clients show interest in your property, ensure you screen them all thoroughly. Ask for credit scores and records, employment verification (current and past employment), rental history, and photo identification to verify they are fit to be your tenants. Ask the chosen tenants to pay their rent and security deposits before moving into your property. Don't listen to flimsy stories, so you don't fall victim of investments scams.

Learn all housing and occupancy rules and adhere to the reasonable ones. Create a waiting list, so as not to lose out on other potential clients while screening some.

4. Promote a stress-free move-in.
As a landlord, it is essential you have move-in policies and procedures. These policies and procedures should centre on creating an excellent landlord-tenant relationship, rules and regulations of occupancy, and the condition of the property ready for move-in.

To create a long-lasting landlord-tenant relationship, ensure you are observant and always ready to attend to the needs of your tenants. Make friendly occupancy terms and conditions, and be prepared to attend to all matters affecting your tenants as regards your property. Create rules that will put your property in good use by the tenants, as well as allow the tenants to enjoy their stays. Be flexible with your standards, but ensure you enforce the rules and regulations strictly and fairly.

Prepare the property and have it ready for move-in. Don't leave any room for complaints from your tenants on the first day. Be prepared to impress your tenants and make their stay memorable.

5. Retain high-income residents.

It is one thing to attract your desired clients; it is another to retain them. As a landlord, you must be on your toes at all times to ensure you don't lose your high-income customers. This can be achieved by paying attention to details and attending to matters promptly. Don't allow your tenants to have a heap of complaints for you at all times.

Keep your tenants informed at all times. When there is any new development regarding the occupancy, ensure you notify your tenants promptly. Don't wait until the last minute; act fast and do things proactively.

It's not all the time that things run smoothly; the stairs may break one day, the door locks may break, or the ceilings may creak. It is your duty as the landlord to prevent all of these things from happening in due time through preventive maintenance. Don't wait until it happens; periodic checks can serve as an eye-opener to potential damage. Fix them when discovered to avoid the next occurrence.

There are times that despite all preventive maintenance, things get faulty. This is due to wear and tear; as a landlord, ensure you have a contingency plan for when this occurs. Have the best handymen and service companies ready to cater for such occurrences. Don't inconvenient your tenants; respond well and put things back in order.

6.   Increase your rent, only and only if it is favourable.

To create sustainable wealth through real estate investments, you need to increase your cash flows from time to time and generate more profits. Increasing rent is one way to go about it. The problem here is, an increase in rent can lead to the risk of losing a good tenant. It goes without saying that, in as much as you want to generate more income, only increase the rent when it is favourable.

There are specific market periods that support an increase in rent. When rentals are in high demands and market competition has reduced, an increase in rent is favourable. Study the trends and know when to propose and implement a rent increase. Verify the market support before offering a rent increase to avoid losing your clients.

Communicate and present facts to your tenants to support your proposal. You can show your tenants property taxes, property insurance, and maintenance expenses to back your claims. This allows your tenants to reason along with you and invariably agree with you.

Give incentives as a way of appreciating the agreement to the increase. You can install new security systems, add new appliances, and do some refurbishing. Ensure the increase is gradual and frequent to allow the tenants to pay without trouble. A significant increment at once may lead to complaints and an ultimate loss of tenants.

7. Expect and handle special problems.

It's not all the time that things are smooth and rosy. Your tenants may suddenly face certain setbacks like divorce, accidents, ill health, unemployment, or bankruptcy, amongst others. It is important you show empathy and understanding to your tenants' plights at this point.

It is a good thing to show understanding, but remember, this is a business and it must be handled as such. Ensure that the rents are still paid despite all. You can suggest help from social workers, charities, or other means of financial support. If it is too difficult for your distressed tenants, negotiate a voluntary move-out.

If it comes to the point of eviction, do it the right way - that is, legally. Do it from a legal standpoint; put together a written notice of the legitimate action taken. There must be time to cure the breach of contract and time to prepare for a hearing. Allow the tenants to have defences to be fair in your dealings. There must be a notice of days the tenants have to move out before being forcefully evicted.

8. Maintain your property.

In becoming a successful landlord, it is crucial you manage your property to avoid wear and tear, complaints from your tenants, or the ultimate loss of tenants.

Maintenance is vital in the rental business. This minimises complaints from your tenants and attracts potential residents. Enhance the value of your property through maintenance. There are different forms of maintenance that can be carried out in property management.

- **Preventive and Corrective Maintenance:** This involves the repairs and replacements of faulty appliances or parts of the property. It also comprises fixing of places with the potential of getting faulty in due time. Doors, windows, electrical appliances, floors, are in this category.

- **Custodial Maintenance:** This form of maintenance focuses on keeping the property neat and tidy. It involves hiring a waste collection service, a cleaning service, and so on.
- **Cosmetic Maintenance:** This is the maintenance of the property's looks. The floors and grounds are inspected, peeling walls are repainted, carpet stains are removed or carpets are replaced, burnt countertops are replaced
- **Safety and Security Maintenance:** This maintenance is aimed at improving the safety and security of your tenants. Repair broken stairs, lightning, doors, windows, or latches. Ensure security systems like smoke alarms are intact. For potential threats to safety and security, ask tenants to contact you and respond appropriately.

9. Plan for a smooth Move-out.

There is no lifetime rental agreement, so it is expected that your tenants' contracts come to an end. To ensure this process is smooth and without hassle, ask for a written notice at least thirty days or more before the due date.

A damage inspection should be carried out a few days before or on the day of the move-out. Ask for damage claims if there are damages caused by the tenants. Ensure you are professional and maintain a good relationship with your tenants until the very end.

After the move-out, start preparing for vacancies and accommodation of new tenants.

10. Increase your cash flows.

As discussed earlier, in chapter seven, there are several ways of managing and increasing your cash flows. Ensure you implement those methods to increase the cash flows needed to maintain your property and make more profits. You can also invest in refinancing with your current cash flows to gain more and achieve sustainable wealth.

Becoming a successful landlord isn't a "day job" as it requires many efforts, dedication, proper planning, and patience. Learn the ropes of becoming a successful landlord and apply what you know. You are assured of achieving your dreams of sustainable wealth in the real estate business.

Chapter Thirteen

Exit Strategies: Have Varying Options

There are many people out there testing the waters of real estate investment without knowing the rudiments. Little wonder, they have experienced many failed investment deals. Successful real estate investors are knowledgeable and informed about investment deals and options to exit. This has helped them achieve sustainable wealth in the real estate business. As a beginner in the real estate business, you should learn about having several exit strategies before you begin investing.

This chapter will enlighten you on the several options under "Exit Strategies" you can choose from when investing. It also focuses on the factors that determine your choice of an exit strategy and factors that can allow the exit strategy not to go as planned. Get your pen and book and learn the secrets of exit strategies.

What Is a Real Estate Exit Strategy?
From the name, it can be implied that a real estate exit strategy is a plan in which the real estate investor intends to remove him/herself from a real estate

investing deal. An exit strategy is a proposed plan of what the real estate investor will do with the investment property.

There are several exit strategies that you as a real estate investor can employ when investing in a deal. You can either have the exit strategy as an original investment plan or decide on it as things unfold during the process of investing. The best method is to have an exit strategy along with your investment plan.

So many real estate investors have failed to identify the importance of exit strategies, which is evident in their investment plans with no exit options.

Why is Real Estate Exit Strategy Important?
Establishing an appropriate real estate exit strategy will not only provide you as a real estate investor with a plan of action, but it will also minimise risks. As a real estate investor, you can evaluate potential exit strategies before purchasing investment properties; this will expose you to the risks associated with the investment and help you avoid them.

Having a specific exit strategy is vital to the success of your investment, as the right exit option will result in maximised profits and sustainable wealth. It's always safer to enter a real estate investment deal with a clear picture of the profit you can get from the real estate property when exiting from the investing deal. This implies that having a financial goal and an exit strategy can save you a spot of money and generate long-lasting wealth in your real estate business.

In cases of unexpected emergencies, a real estate exit strategy can serve as a way out of that emergency. You may be in dire need of cash; with a real estate exit strategy you can sell the property faster and cash out.

As a real estate investor, you should be looking into expanding your investment coast and building your investment portfolio. With an exit strategy, you get to learn how to manage these different investment belongings. You will also know how to react and the way forward when an investment isn't giving you your desired outcome.

To reduce the potential risks and increase the profits in your real estate investments, you must understand the essence of having an exit option. In generating sustainable wealth through real estate business, you must identify, understand and implement the various real estate exit strategies available.

Various Real Estate Exit Strategy Available
Having the right ideology about exit strategies will go a long way in achieving your dreams of sustainable wealth.

1. Fix-and-Flip

This real estate exit strategy is a typical profit-generating plan, as it allows you as a real estate investor to sell the real estate property at full market value. It involves purchasing investment properties at low market value, putting them under repair, renovating them, and then selling them for more than the original investment costs - that is, the purchase price plus repair costs.

As a real estate investor willing and seeking to execute this exit strategy option, you must be aware of market trends and demands. You must also have the capacity to increase the value of your real estate investment properties.

2. Buy-and-Hold

This exit strategy is ideal if, as a real estate investor, you are looking to build up equity in a real estate property. It has a similar option to that of fix-and-flip. The difference here is that instead of selling the renovated property, as a real estate investor, you can choose to hold it for some time and rent it out to generate cash flow for your real estate business.

As appreciation and equity increase the value of the property, it can be put on the market to be sold for a profit. You must also know market trends here to achieve your purpose.

3. Wholesaling

In this type of exit strategy, as a real estate investor, you act as the middleman between a property seller and a property buyer. Basically, as a real estate wholesaler, you will scout for cheap property from distressed buyers and quickly sell for a profit margin. After the purchase, you then place the investment property under a purchase contract and then sell this contract to the buyer for a small profit.

This exit strategy is implemented in investments wherein you need to end the deal because it saves you time.

4. Seller Financing

This exit strategy is employed when exiting an investment deal which continues to produce a profit. In this investment plan, the seller finances the real estate investing deal and acts as a bank. Then, there is an exchange of promissory note indicating an interest rate and a repayment schedule between the buyer and the seller.

This exit strategy is beneficial to real estate sellers as they are awarded monthly payments to cover the mortgage loan. They also get to have a nice increased return on the investments due to interest.

5. Rent to Own (Lease Option)

In this type of exit strategy, you are allowed to rent your property to a tenant, with the option to purchase it after a set period. You may save a part of the monthly payments towards the purchase of the property.

The above types of exit strategies can be employed in any investment deal as desired.

Factors Influencing the Choice of an Exit Strategy

You can decide on whatever exit strategy you want for a specific investment. However, certain factors will affect your decision. These factors will help you determine the suitable exit strategy for a particular investment deal. They are:

- Short-term and long-term goals
- Experience in real estate
- Closing time
- Sale price
- Value of the property
- Terms and condition of the property
- Market trends
- Market demands
- Available financing options
- The profit potential of the investment
- Location of the property

Understanding these factors will allow a real estate investor to determine which of the real estate exit strategies they should follow.

Factors That Can Demerit an Exit Strategy

As a real estate investor, you should know that an exit strategy may not go as planned due to certain factors. These factors are:

- Depreciation
- Loss of rent as a result of tenancy issues
- Unforeseen maintenance expenses, which may cancel out profits
- Decreased value of the property as a result of poor property management
- When a property cannot be flipped as a result of no demand, failed escrow, or backing out of the partnership by a partner

Having more than one exit strategy is the key to solving the above issue. As a beginner in the real estate business, it is best to know when to opt out of an investment deal, when it is profitable to sell, and why it is important to have several exit strategies at your disposal.

Chapter Fourteen

How to Prevent Investment Scams

Real estate is not an easy business; finding the right property, organising the proper funding, and managing a rental take a lot of time and effort. And just like in any business, there are people who want to scam you out of your hard work.

This chapter focuses on real estate investment scams - the various types, how to identify them, what to do when you do, and how to prevent yourself from falling for those scams.

The art of scamming has evolved over time, and the more types of investment, the bigger and broader the scam. Con artists are becoming more sophisticated in their scamming methods, thus increasing their detriments. No one is immune to investment scams, but you can be careful enough to avoid falling for them.

What are real estate investment scams?

Scams are fraudulent activities carried out with the ultimate goal of deception for an ulterior motive. There are certain people who derive pleasure in allowing others to work for money and deceiving them to get away with that money. For real estate, investment scams are aimed at duping real estate investors, buyers, and sellers into investment deals that are detrimental to them.

Real estate investment scams have been in existence since just about the time real estate investments were discovered. Scammers in the real estate field mostly target beginners and not-so-experienced investors. It is undeniable that what you don't know, you can't question. This principle is what real estate investment scammers employ in carrying out their evil plans.

Real estate investment scams involve a fraud proposing investment deals that are fake, detrimental and aimed to make you lose your wealth. Promises are made but not kept, what is being paid for isn't done or carried out, fake qualifications, disappearing after collecting rents, and security deposits of property not owned, are all characteristics portrayed by real estate investment frauds.

As a beginner in real estate business, you have to be vigilant and observant, know the signs, and watch out for them. There are remedies for real estate investment scams. Criminal prosecution, rescission of contracts, punitive damages, and internal revenue service penalties are examples of such remedies.

To have a better understanding of real estate investment scams, you must know the various types of investment frauds available.

Types of Real Estate Scams

1. Loan Modification Scams:

This real estate investment scam is a notorious one, as it preys on many investors, especially beginners. It is something that a real estate investor like you should be wary of. The typical victims of this scam are homeowners who are struggling to pay a mortgage or are facing foreclosure. A scammer will act as a 'lender' and will offer to 'modify' the loan so that the owner pays lesser amounts. They may even assure a 'guarantee' of protection from foreclosure. But of course, the owner has to pay a fee, usually an upfront fee - a fraud alert. The investor will also be asked to send personal information, including a bank account number, to the scammer.

These scammers are incredibly cunning. Some scammers will have a website with a government logo or even that end in ".gov". However, they are avoidable. Do not get involved with third parties when it comes to a mortgage. Deal with your mortgage company and them only, even when facing difficulty in paying.

The fraud alerts of loan modifications are demanding upfront payments and asking for personal information. It is illegal for a company to ask for upfront payments; make sure you know that! Also, beware of anyone or any agency asking for your bank account information. Chances are, they want to scam you!

2. Rental Scams:

Investors interested in buying a rental will first turn to the internet for their property search. This is just pure fact, and the actual number of investors who turn to the internet is over 90%. Equipped with this knowledge, scam artists turn to the Internet as well. What they then do is select an actual listing, that is not theirs, and post it on their website - or even on commonly used sites like Craigslist. The craftier computer scammers may even hack the site of the original listing and replace the written information with some of their own. The investor is then asked to wire the payment to a third party.

These real estate investment scammers do not necessarily need the Internet. The more old-fashioned con artists will offer property at a very low price. During an open house, they will ask interested buyers to fill out an application and pay some fees. Then, if they contact you or you contact them, they will tell you that your application has been rejected.

Whether the scammer is online or not, an investor will be asked to wire the payment, no matter the kind of payment. The scammer will demand payment, even if you two have not met yet or signed any legal documents. These investors will also claim they are out of the country - another warning to be aware of. All of these are big no-no's you should watch out for. To learn how to report rental scams officially, read this.

3. Mortgage Syndication Scams:

A mortgage is said to be in syndication when there is a marriage of equals, people with money to spare, and people with a solid, vetted business plan/venture. Every party is aware of such marriage risks and can function due to the diligence required to ascertain their level of risk.

All the mortgage syndication frauds involve the cloaking of asymmetry or risk in an unequal relationship. This means one of the parties has a lot more information than the other. One of the parties will generally know more about the business than the other. One party will be more educated than the other. One party will have more access to professionals than the other.

In most cases, the mortgage syndication company will be offering an investor that has never had any additional information or exposure to the investment, a higher level.

4. Seminar Scams:

The one thing all real estate investment scams have in common, aside from scamming investors, is that they put on the pretence of wanting to help an investor and end up duping them. As a beginner in the real estate business, you are susceptible to such pretence, because of the eagerness to break even. In seminar scams, the scammer might provide actual help as a form of bait in achieving their aim.

Just like loan modification scams, seminar scams soared during the housing bubble. This scam is primarily a workshop by an 'expert'. The expert will provide gullible investors with "get-rich-quick" tips, some of them being actually valuable and factual. This unconsciously plants seeds of trust the investor has for the expert. Then, the scammer will offer investors a property that is available "for a limited time" or additional classes that cost thousands of dollars.

If investors buy one of the limited properties hastily, they may not be able to review the property as accurately as they usually would. Then, only after the purchase, the investor realises that the property may be flawed in some ways and has taken part in a bad investment.

Falling for the second trap is just as detrimental to the investor. The course turns out to offer investors with basic and repetitive information. This leaves them feeling frustrated since they spent thousands of dollars on a course that provided so little.

Once an investor becomes entangled in one of these real estate investment scams, it can become difficult to get out of. Why? Well, by signing an agreement document with the scammer, the investor is limited with legal action against the scammer.

To avoid these real estate investment scams, do your research. Research the 'expert', the property, and courses they may present. The research will also help you find certified and trustworthy experts and any companies they are affiliated with.

5. Title Scams:

Last on the list of most common real estate investment scams, is title fraud. It is the least common of the ones mentioned on the list, but it can be just as or more destructive. This scam could potentially result in identity theft.

This is how it works - a scammer will use false documents to pose as a home seller. The scammer will recommend to buyers not to purchase title insurance. This leaves the buyer with a detrimental investment.

The scammer may also request personal information from the buyer in order to sell.

Title scams can be avoided through the purchase of title insurance. This helps to protect the buyer from the false impersonation of the seller. The title insurance company will verify the deal and search for any mortgage attached to the property.

The above real estate investment scams are quite common, among others. These investment frauds are common and similar to the real deal, hence, can be mistaken for an authentic deal. Learn to distinguish them properly and be prepared to avoid them

How to Identify Real Estate Investment Scams

There are many real estate investors out there. Some are testing out their luck in the business of real estate, some have purposes they want to achieve with it, and some others are out there to reap the benefit of others' efforts. To avoid being a victim of real estate investment scams, you must be able to identify them when you see them. This way, you can run away from them as far as possible.

Many investment frauds try to mimic the real deal so you don't suspect them. However, since it isn't the authentic deal, certain phrases or clauses stand out, hence pointing them out as scams. Some investment scams are too similar to real investment deals, and this may cause you to miss out on real and significant deals. With proper research and knowing how not to fall for investment scams, you can make it out unscathed.

Phrases and clauses that can be identified in common investment deals:

- 'No money down' mortgage deals
- Deals with unrealistic guarantees
- Deals that sell the dream, rather than sharing the knowledge
- Deals that negotiate by creating a sense of scarcity
- 'Risk-free'
- 'Magic'
- 'Secrets'
- 'Bullet-proof'
- 'Get rich quick'
- 'Bearers bonds'
- 'Advance fee' on mortgage loans
- 'Judgement-proof'
- 'Nevada Corporations' outside Nevada, among others.

With the above phrases and clauses, you can spot an investment fraud easily and prevent yourself from falling for them.

How to Avoid Falling for Investment Scams

Ensure that you know what investment scams are and that you can identify them and the various types available. It is crucial you learn how to prevent yourself from falling for investment frauds. This way, you don't get to see that ugly aspect of real estate business.

Rules and regulations regarding investment scams differ from state to state. Having the right information is vital and acting on it is the best solution. When you are faced with an investment scam, these are the things to do:

1. Research and gather the correct information.

Knowledge is power only when it's at your fingertips. We are in the jet age, where things have been made easy. As a real estate investor, you must be a researcher and have the ability to gather information before investing. This is to your advantage as you will have an eye opener into what you are getting involved in.

Before investing in any real estate deal, be sure to do proper research. Know all the information about it. Know why the seller wants to sell and at what price. Know the market value of a property and the potential profits that can be generated from it, before you secure such deals.

2. Check for certifications, licensure and all other types of credentials.

Phony investors portray themselves as the real deal, only they don't have the necessary credentials to back their claims. As a real estate investor, don't start negotiating a deal until you have verified some of the necessary credentials involved. This will serve as a guarantee that you are on the right track. Check out all property certificates and licensure as well as those of the investor, buyer, or seller.

Know the credit score and records of your potential tenants before leasing out your property. When you want to hire a caretaker or a property management company, check out their reviews from previous clients and ask for certifications and licenses.

3. Consult professionals on all issues.

One mistake that too many beginners like you in the real estate business make is having an 'I-Know-What-I-am-doing' mentality. Since you are new, not experienced, and trying to find your feet, it is in your best interest to have successful and experienced real estate investors as mentors or allies. When you have such persons as mentors or allies, you are sure to have a good backing.

Consult these professionals on issues related to real estate investments. There are also professionals like real estate attorneys and tax advisors that you should consult when the need arises. Don't live in your shell, believing you can achieve it on your own, until you fall victim of investment frauds. Rather, ask questions of the right people.

4. Be objective and rational.

One of the crucial qualities a real estate investor must possess is being clearheaded. This quality is vital in investing in the real estate business. Being objective in your dealings will allow you avoid some investment scams. With objectivity, you can think from a neutral point of view, weighing all options. You also make decisions based on facts and figures and not mere hearsay.

Being rational will enable you to avoid giving in to emotional sways from investment frauds. You must be level-headed and composed. Hold conversations with confidence and don't be moved by unnecessary and false claims.

5. Don't be in haste.

Real estate is a long-term investment; hence, there is plenty of time to secure a great deal, purchase property, rent it out to your desired customers, or sell when it is profitable. Though some deals are time-bound, there is still no need to be in a rush. It is safe for you to take your time to gather knowledge and experience before investing in some deals.

There are many real estate investment traps out there, and by taking your time, you can avoid them. Dig into everything surrounding the deal and if you are faced with potential scams, abandon such deal. Take your time to investigate the seller, buyer, or lender.

6. Make it official.

Nothing is official until you put your signature on it. A deal isn't secured yet until you have documents in your name bearing your signature. Don't trust the words of people; rather allow them to put their words into writing and have it bound by the law.

Don't let yourself be swayed by sweet talkers that a legal document isn't needed. Ensure it is provided; otherwise, let go of such deals.

7. Do your homework yourself.

Regardless of what the deal is, as a real estate investor, it is advisable you do the work yourself. Delegating it may backfire. Check out properties yourself; visit the location and the local government yourself; cross-check what was written in the contract to what you can see.

As a beginner in the real estate business, it is essential you do all of this yourself. You are the only ONE that can have the best interest of your investment at heart, don't let others jeopardise it.

8. Ask questions and satisfy your curiosity.
Finally, when any question comes to your mind about the property or deal, ask. Ensure that you know everything about what you plan to get involved with, whether it's a property, deal, data, or anything else. Pique your interest and satisfy your curiosity.

There are also times you need to trust your gut instincts. This should be done after you have satisfied your curiosity. With all questions asked, you can be assured of what you are doing.

Real estate investment scams are real and it would be devastating to fall victim. This goes without saying that, you have to be careful and ensure you don't fall into such traps.

Thank you and I hope you enjoy this audiobook, the only thing is I ask is if you could please leave a review after listening.

Chapter Fifteen

You've Got It, Now KEEP It

Finally, it's the last chapter in this book about creating sustainable wealth through real estate. If you have read the whole book to this point, you deserve a round of applause. The journey of a thousand miles begins with just one step. You have embarked on the journey of long-lasting wealth through real estate and reading this book is a huge step to reach your destination.

You have learned a lot about the real estate business and how you can generate sustainable wealth through it. You know the practical guides, tips, and principles needed to aide you in reaching your dreams. You have been exposed to how to maximise your gain, explore various exit strategies, and avoid investment scams. Now is the time to learn how to keep your real estate investments, so you don't end up losing all you have gained.

This chapter focuses on the things to do to protect your property and investments. It also serves as a guide on how to avoid liabilities or legal issues surrounding the real estate business. All in all, you are going to learn how to treasure your investments. Do read and enjoy!

Real estate investments may be long-term, but if not properly managed or maintained, there may have short-term challenges. It is in your best interest as a real estate investor that you take proper care to ensure you don't lose your hard work, diligence, persistence, and patience in one swoop. As a beginner in the real estate business, having learned a lot up to this point, you've got it, now KEEP it!

The following are ways to keep your real estate investments:

1. Make your tenants your priority.

If you are investing in the rental business, your tenants are your primary source of income, so make them your priority. The rent generated from your property serves as a consistent cash flow for investing in real estate. To keep it up, ensure your tenants are happy and satisfied with your services.

Attend to complaints promptly and come up with policies that will be beneficial to your tenants.

2. A Property Manager will do the trick.

Property management has been discussed in a previous chapter, and you can recall the forms of property management discussed. As a beginner in the real estate business, self-management was recommended. Now that there are many properties to look after, it is safe to say a property manager will do the trick.

Recruit a competent and reliable property manager or caretaker. A property management company can also be beneficial, drop ending on your wants and resources. This will save you the stress and hassle of managing several properties.

3. Manage and maintain your properties.

The most important method of keeping your investments is to manage and maintain your properties. This is how you can increase the value of your property and attract your desired clients. Maintenance is critical and can go a long way in generating sustainable wealth in your real estate investments.

Make improvements to your property where necessary and boost its features. Conversions are good, rehabilitation, and renovations are even better.

5. Insurance protects your properties.

One sure way to ensure you don't lose much as a real estate investor is INSURANCE. Avoid losses from natural disasters, accidents, and litigation by insuring your properties. Invest in a reliable insurance company with a great offer. Ignorance is deadly; insurance is reviving!

6. Put your investments under a corporation.

To reduce liability and to ensure the protection of your properties, you should invest in a corporation. Register your investments under LLC and be assured of little or no liability.

7. Know when to call it quits.

While you can leverage on debt to acquire properties at a lower price to their original market price, it's best if you are careful. If not careful, you may acquire an investment with too many debt payments. Know when to use leverage to your advantage and know when to call it quits.

9. Prepare an "Exit Strategy."

With every investment deal you secure, there must be an exit strategy for when you decide to opt out. Always have an exit strategy ready to be executed as soon as you give the signal. Review the different exit strategies available and choose the one that's suitable for the deal at hand.

11. Face issues of cash flow squarely.

There are times when problems may arise in regards to your cash flows; to protect your investments, face them squarely. Take bold steps and measures to ensure that the challenges are solved and you are back on track.

12. Work with the local authorities

To ensure the smooth running of your real estate business, it is imperative you work with the local authorities. Know the various organisations available in that locality and ensure you create a strong rapport with their representatives.

Visit the local government to learn more about the vicinity and how you can increase the value of your property.

It is essential you know how to keep your investments safe and not fall victim of fraud, scam, or bankruptcy. Don't lose your wealth; instead generate more!

Stock Market Investing For Beginners 101: The Ultimate Guide To Stock Market Investing & Trading For Beginners - Discover How To Easily Invest & Make Money Trading Stocks And Dominate The Market Like A Pro!

Jordan Priesley

INTRODUCTION

Over the years, people - especially those who have no clue what the stock market is - have looked at it with suspicion. Getting them to invest in the stock market is like trying to sell ice to an Eskimo. It is virtually impossible. The moment you meet them physically or online and want to talk stocks with them, they start giving you one hundred and one reasons why the venture is risky and could collapse at any time. The fluidity of the market doesn't help matters, but like all business, there are always risks involved in trading. What makes a business stand the test of time is to know how to adjust to fit the market environment and demands.

Reading a bunch of articles online, getting books that explain stock broking in a broader sense, watching tutorial videos, and staring at pie charts, bar charts, and all manner of charts without knowing if they are important or not has been the downfall of many people. All you get from putting in so much effort are just bits and pieces of information. If you cannot see the big picture, you are as good as getting stuck in tar. The harder you struggle, the more stuck you get.

To a large extent, life consists of overcoming the problems we encounter in our attempts to achieve our purposes. Along with the easy problems in life are many enormously complex and difficult ones. These would be considerably less difficult if our notions about how the world works were more reliable.

It is comforting to have reliable knowledge to deal with problem and situations situations that have straightforward, linear cause-and-effect relationships. For example, fixing a flashlight that no longer works by replacing the batteries poses little challenge to our knowledge of cause and effect. But, approaching complex problems with an overly simplistic linear mindset often makes matters worse instead of better.

Based on an analysis of the work of people, especially scientists, who have been extremely successful in solving complex problems, I have learned three lessons that are important to a better understanding of knowing:

1. Reality as we know it is just our perception of it — a kind of map of reality, not the true territory of reality.
2. Action is an integral part of cause-and-effect loops, with purpose playing a critical - and often overlooked role.
3. Identifying the strongly held assumptions (beliefs) that influence what we perceive and how we determine our actions in the world is vitally important in opening us up to perceiving new feedback information and to faster knowledge improvement.

Putting these lessons into practice takes conscious effort because much of our life experience has been dealing with the outside world as independent components of reality for which one-way, or linear, cause-and-effect thinking is adequate.

The Loop
The perceiving - acting - knowing system can be visualized as a loop of intimately related components. A useful understanding of how this system functions requires a focus on the loop as a whole and not on the components in isolation.

As noted by the psychologist Hadley Cantril, perceiving, acting, and knowing are interdependent processes. Nevertheless, a discussion of the Loop requires some starting point. For convenience, we will begin at the point where an individual is trying to achieve a purpose within the context of the perceived world "out there."

Purposes
Purposes are personal. They are the outcomes we, as individuals, seek from the actions we take. (This is not to say we always get what we seek.) The great bulk of our purposes are mundane. Consider all the specific, detailed purposes and related actions taken in driving to work — from a small, or low–level, action such as moving the steering wheel a little to the left or right to counteract a crosswind, so the car stays on our intended course. Some larger, or higher-level, purposes of driving to work would include: why you work (survival? self-fulfillment? enjoyment?) and why you have a particular job (steppingstone to a better job? prestige? power?). It quickly becomes evident that we function within a

hierarchy of purposes, with higher purposes guiding, or setting lower purposes.

Being cognizant of higher-level purposes is especially relevant to business wealth creation. An example is given of the decision of a Japanese pharmaceutical company's top management to align the firm's mission statement (purpose) with the higher-order purpose of genuinely helping patients that were widely shared by employees. One result was significantly improved corporate financial performance.

Studies of brain activity suggest that many of the common things we do are not associated with brain areas that are responsible for awareness or consciousness. We operate much of the time as if on autopilot (Gazzaniga, Ivry, and Mangun, 2008). This is highly functional, and indeed necessary.

Otherwise, our consciousness would be overwhelmed by minutiae — perceptual noise. Evolution has equipped us to do things much more quickly than we could if everything required conscious mental processing. Many actions would be impossible. Think of all the things that require virtually instantaneous "muscle memory," such as getting out of bed, walking, or typing.

But being on autopilot has its downside, too. Consider two economists given the task or purpose of evaluating whether minimum wage legislation is good or bad for the economy. One economist is a believer in free markets, and the other believes government regulation is necessary to prevent or fix market deficiencies. Because of their core assumptions, they are on different automatic pilot programs, and their expectations are already set to a large degree (Olson, Roese, and Zanna, 1996). The data they choose to consider (and ignore), the periods covered, and the forms of analysis employed for the lower-level research purpose of evaluating the economic impact of minimum wage legislation are most likely to be biased.

Economists (and other inquirers) who have a genuine, higher-level purpose of better understanding cause and effect need to explicitly guard against being guided by their automatic thinking and acting templates. Such researchers would be well served by, at an early stage, explicitly working creatively to overcome the heavy hand of often - unconscious beliefs.

Perceptions

Any discussion of perceptions raises the age-old philosophical question, "What is the reality?" (Madden, 1991). Thinking that there is a pure, independent reality needs to be replaced with the concept that reality is dependent on an individual's experience and current knowledge base, such that each of us is a participant in perceptions of what is "out there." This also helps put into practice one of the hallmark criteria of science, namely, that all knowledge is tentative and subject to revision.

In the 1940s and 1950s, Adelbert Ames Jr. and his colleagues initiated a paradigm shift away from the view of perception as a passive response to the external environment and toward the view of perception as a process actively carried out by the individual (Bamberger, 2006). Ames was frequently labeled a genius due to his path-breaking research in visual perception at the Dartmouth Eye Institute. Ames and John Dewey often exchanged ideas on Dewey's transactional approach to knowledge as it is related to perception (Cantril, 1960).

The Ames Demonstrations were a series of ingenious laboratory experiments that illustrated the dominating influence of observers' strongly held assumptions. For example, assumptions that floors are level, windows rectangular, bigger is closer, and the like, are particularly strong because of our extensive experience with actions being successful based on the validity of these kinds of assumptions. When an experiment falsifies a strongly held assumption, we nevertheless construct a visual "reality" that conforms to what we "know" to be true.

The Ames Demonstrations in visual perception were instrumental in showing that purpose, perception, and action are all parts of a single connected system. These experiments strongly suggest that perception is never a sure thing, never an absolute revelation of "what is." Rather, what we see is a prediction — our construction designed to give us the best possible bet for carrying out our purposes in action.

We make these bets based on our experience. When we have a great deal of relevant and consistent experience to relate to stimulus patterns the probability of success of our prediction (perception) as a guide to action is extremely high, and we tend to have a feeling of surety. When our experience is limited or inconsistent, the reverse holds. . . .

Perception is a functional affair based on action, experience and probability. The thing perceived is an inseparable part of the function of perceiving, which in turn includes all aspects of the total process of living.

The interdependent processes that contribute to visual perception are analogous to the components of the Loop, which are best viewed as cross-linked together in a system that, for the most part, operates simultaneously as opposed to a mechanistic step-by-step procedure.

It is important to keep in mind when you are investing in the stock market that it functions as a system. Our knowledge base has a significant impact on how we see the world and how we react to situations in the stock market as well as life as a whole. We must remember that knowledge is always incomplete and situations are complex. We can't always simplify and make assumptions based solely on our own individual knowledge bases.

This guide will break everything down into small bits. I won't be going around in a circle. I will strike the nail on the head and make my point as clear as possible. I will also avoid bringing up equations that would give you a headache. Parts of this guide are designed in a question and answer format. The questions will be probable ones.

It is going to be a rich guide that will answer all your questions and prop up the zeal and confidence in you to invest in the stock market.

SECTION 1: STOCK MARKET – THE BASICS OF INVESTING

INVESTING

Simply put, investing is utilizing your money in such a way that it earns more money for you after you have removed the capital and expenditures. Something beautiful about investing is that you know the money is working for you 24 hours a day, seven days a week - and it doesn't get tired. All that money needs is someone who understands it and knows how to invest it in the proper channel.

This section will point out one thing, the art of investing your money in something which may not necessarily be the stock market. Come along; it will get more exciting and expository as we go.

Why should you invest your money?
Inflation is currently the biggest enemy every economy is fighting. In economics, inflation is defined as a general increase in prices of goods and services and a fall in the purchasing value of money. Put in layman's terms, inflation has to do with an increase in the prices of commodities and services we regularly get while the value of money takes a dip. No one and nothing is exempted from the impact of inflation as it hits everything that makes life comfortable.

Goods and services that people bought for a cheaper price years ago are now more expensive due to inflation. The value of $10 in the year 1920, according to The Bureau of Labour Statistics, is worth nearly $120 today. That is over one thousand percent inflation. It shows one thing; it was easier to live on $10 in the year 1920 than it is today. The prices of goods and services valued at that amount increased with time. It shows that the value of $10 and its purchasing power decreased geometrically while the value of the goods and services it can purchase increased.

Inflation is a factor we have no control over, as the price of food, rent, transportation, electricity, cable, and other necessities will continue to climb up the scale. In the same manner, the goods and services purchasable and affordable by $10 will continue to decrease. There is every tendency that $10 of today will be worth a lot in twenty or thirty years. It is an inescapable truth.

What does inflation do?
Inflation, like climate change, does not only affect the lives we are leading now but also our dreams and aspirations for the future. Let's take this simple analogy:

Imagine you are in a race of exchanging batons and at the end when you hand over your baton, you get to choose your dream house, car, or even a vacation. Whether you arrive first or last is ruled out. The important thing is you get the prize as long as you hand over your baton.

You've been in the race for a while now; you are running out of breath and putting every last ounce of your energy into passing the baton. You can see others passing too, at the verge of passing theirs in front of you, while some others are running beside you. Still others gave up and stopped the race halfway, but you keep pushing.

Suddenly, another runner draws your attention. You look at him and he points to the ground. You check only to find out that your shoes became untied in the course of the race. You go down and begin to tie your shoes but immediately notice something; the ground you are on is moving backward.

Confused by this, you put your hand on the ground to inspect more closely. You discover that the ground is moving backward! The movement is slow, but it is moving! You lift your head to confirm if the same thing is happening everywhere. You even take a few steps backward to check it out. After checking it a couple of times, you realize you've wasted time looking at the ground. You spring back up on your feet and enter into the race again. This time, you push yourself harder. You have to get to the finish live.

This analogy describes inflation. We get moved backward, financially, little by little. We all know it exists but choose to ignore it. All we do is work harder for our dreams to become a reality but we don't realize that we get pushed back and farther from achieving our dreams by inflation. If the cost of our dreams today is $250,000, it will cost $290,000 in five years and $350,000 in ten years. In twenty years, it would have tripled.

The good news is this; inflation can be fought! This is by learning how to invest.

Investing – The Sure Way to Fight Inflation

People are continuously divided into two groups by inflation: the investors, who are above inflation, and the "non-investors". The investors who can invest above inflation accumulate wealth and become richer. Those who are scared of investing create poverty and become poor. As unfortunate as it seems, this is the story of a lot of people. They forget that there is a thin line between being poor and being rich and staying rich is investment. Time and consistency is also a determining factor. When you invest constantly, you tend to save more, and inflation doesn't get to you. Not investing and depending on your salary as your only source of income increases your wealth on the negative side, below inflation.

What will happen if you fail to invest?

When you get a 5% increase per year or a 0.4% increase per month or a 0.01% increase in the costs of goods and services, you find it impossible to notice it. So it is safe to say that inflation can be an invisible enemy. You don't get to see its impact on a day to day basis.

Retirement is the portal that opens you up to the full impact of inflation. You realize that having not fought it, you are left at its mercy and have to keep adjusting and re-adjusting until you are swimming in the murky waters of poverty. Since you do not have enough money for failing to invest, your last days are spent financially constrained and a burden to the ones you love the most.

For most organizations and government institutions, the retirement age is pegged at 65 or after 35 years of active service. Now imagine at the age of 65, and you are no longer working. Who pays for your water, food, medicine, electricity, and doctor's visits? Would your pension be able to cover all those mentioned above? Do you see the picture clearly in your mind? No investment, no income coming in, and a lot of expenses waiting to be cleared. A very grim future, if you ask me.

Life expectancy of an average American was pegged at 78.69 years in the year 2016. Now, when you retire at the age of 65, you will need enough funds to keep you going for about 13 or more years. Let's check how much it will cost in estimation. I will be asking some questions which you will answer.
1.   How much will you be spending per month if you retire today?
2.   How much would be coming in as your pension after you retire?

Alright, let's peg your current salary at $8000 per month or $96,000 per year. How many years do you have left before retirement? 15? What's your yearly cost of living? Over $60,000, according to the Bureau of Labour Statistics, is spent annually by an average American family. What do you have left? How much is your pension? Will it be enough to keep you floating when you finally retire?

It is my sincere hope that after answering the questions above, the amount you see ends up scaring you into taking action immediately. You can easily delay investing; you can even go ahead and ignore it, but the tradeoff from your actions at the end of the day is extremely painful.

I work with a good organization that gives me pay raise every year.
Congratulations! I am sure you work hard and are deserving of your yearly pay raise. This doesn't take you away from the need to invest, though. The "money-illusion" as it is called gives you the tendency to think of the money in its absolute amount instead of its purchasing power.

The Money Illusion
Let me tell you a story to buttress this point:

John works for a construction company. Being active with a lot of energy is something that he is proud of. Now, because of his ability, skills, and endurance, he gets a lot of job offers. John also works two to three jobs every day in the same company. He has one for the morning, another for the afternoon, and a third one in the evening.

John earns around $15 in the morning. This he spends on his favorite breakfast which is from KFC. 8 pc. chicken and soda to wash it down. The meal costs him $15, which is just enough.

John got a 10% raise in salary a year later. This increased his pay to $22 daily. John was happy that he would be able to save an extra $7. He was delighted with himself.

But check out his surprise when he went to KFC the following morning for his favorite meal. There was also an increase in the price of the chicken and soda bringing everything to a total of $20. John is happy to get a raise, so instead of being turned away by the price, he still goes ahead and makes the purchase. That means reducing his savings to just two dollars.

The above is a perfect example of the absolute amount versus its purchasing power. John got the raise quite all right, but the price of his meal also increased. That means instead of being richer as he had thought he would be with the $7, he only got richer by $2 - which isn't much. John was fortunate to have a raise that is higher than inflation.

A Raise Lower Than the Rise in Inflation
There could be a more upsetting situation at the end of the day, too. This is when inflation jumps higher than the raise in pay given. And unfortunately, for the majority of workers, an annual pay increase does not cover the rising cost of living.

Let's look at another analogy:

We won't be using John again this time. Let's look at James (yeah, James could be the twin brother to John. It is my story). James works in the same company as John, and they are best of buddies (apart from being twins). Both of them earn $15 every morning and both of them always buy their meals from KFC. At just about the same time as John, James got a raise too. However, his wage *was increased to $19. It didn't matter to James. A raise is a raise, all the same, so he was happy with the little increment.*

James decides to go to KFC with John that day. James also ordered the same meal John ordered. Handing his money to the cashier, he waited for his receipt and meal. Here is the shocker. The cashier goes like this:

"Sir, the KFC. 8 pc. chicken and soda is now $20. You only gave me $15."

James was shocked and flabbergasted. He didn't know that his meal had gotten more expensive. He turned around and back to the cashier before lifting his head and staring at the menu. He looked back at the cash in his hand. He looks back at the menu and back at his hand again. He keeps this going until the man standing right behind him told him to hurry up.

Well, poor James had to make a quick decision. He didn't have enough cash on him, and he didn't want to keep the line waiting. So he did the honorable thing. He placed an order for a side of potato wedges and was ravenous just one hour later.

James! Poor James! His pay raise had made him happy, but not for long. He could no longer afford his meal at KFC. This is because of one thing; his pay raise was lower than inflation. What happened to him wasn't a pay raise in the least bit. What he had was a pay-cut.

Again, this is another perfect example of the money illusion.

Increase in Salary

Well, your salary can only be said to have increased - and it is a true increase if and only if it is higher than inflation. As long as there is no increase in your salary, whenever there is inflation, it means only one thing: a pay-cut!

When inflation jumps by 0.2% and your salary increases by 2.0 percent, you are on track. The effect of inflation will not impact you. Therefore, if there is an increase in your pay/salary over the past years and it has always beaten inflation significantly and on a consistent basis, you have a better chance of fighting inflation. Sadly, this is not the case for the majority.

However, one thing remains critical; preparation for retirement. Most of us have some sort of plan for retirement income – and you may think you have set yourself up for success simply by enrolling in your company's standard retirement plan. You may also be relying on government retirement programming that you've been investing in via taxes for decades. Unfortunately, for many, this does not support the quality of living you deserve after many years of hard work.

But, I save money already. Do I really need to invest?

The major difference here is the power of compounding interest. Consistently adding money to a savings account is a great habit! Say you save $1,000 per month for 25 years. You would have saved $300.000. Your bank may pay a small amount of interest, so you can expect a bit more than that. How long could you live a life you love on a total of $300,000? You've worked hard for decades, and likely had to live quite frugally to set aside such a chunk of change each month. Yet you will likely need to work part time throughout your retirement, or rely on family support or public assistance when the money runs out.

Or... you invest that amount each month in the stock market... Remember, the stock market is a place where you can put your money to work creating more money! So, if we assume an average 10% annual return, you would have over $1.7 MILLION in net worth, ensuring a much different lifestyle than you would have achieved from savings alone. Not only could you retire comfortably without worry of burdening your beloved family - you'd likely have a legacy to leave behind as well. It is likely you could live on dividends alone, allowing your money to continue growing throughout retirement.

How do I start investing when I'm already in debt?
Hold up! You are in debt already, and you're thinking of investing? No! You should not think about investing just yet. Your top priority when you are in debt shouldn't be investing. It should be getting out of debt! This is just because every gain you make will be eaten up by the penalties of being in debt. If you earn 10% with your investment and inflation works against you by 5% per year, then you have won the battle.

But note this, if your debt is from your credit card, know that it is more powerful. It works against you by 40% per year (3% per month). Whoa! Look at the figure! It is eight times stronger and more powerful than inflation! This means that even if your income from investments is up to 40% (this is difficult if you put all factors in place and is also not consistent), you end up with nothing - zilch! Everything goes into servicing the debt. This is why you make getting out of debt first your top priority!

How do I get out of debt?
Here are some of the most important and practical things you can do to get out of debt. Remember, this isn't a complete guide to getting out of debt!

You need to start by tracking your debt, recording what is being borrowed and what you're repaying toward your debt.
- A. Always put into the record the amount you pay for your debt and the amount you borrow each month.
- B. Cut down on the amount you borrow each month.
- C. The amount you pay toward your debt each month should increase.

There is this saying that is popular everywhere, "Stop borrowing; leave the credit card at home and pay cash for everything!"

If you have heard the saying before, what are you doing about it? Are you getting involved? Chances are that you are not doing it yet. One reason for this is because you find it uncomfortable to change your old habits. Here is a piece of advice from me; start with A, follow with B, and then with C.

When you put records down about how much you're borrowing and paying back, its reality forces you to face your debt problem. Well, it is the most important decision and step to take in the right direction. Failure to know how big your problem is and how much you have solved from it can lead to you not solving it at all at the end of the day.

Knowing how much you borrow and pay back every month, slowly reduce the amount you are borrowing and also slowly increase, bit by bit, the amount you're paying back. If you borrow $150 every month from different people, try as much as you can to borrow $145 or less this month. That is $5 less, but it is a step. Also, slowly increase the amount you pay back at the end of each month. From paying back only $90, put an effort to start paying $93 per month. The changes might look small, but you are already on your way to becoming debt free.

Keeping record will also keep you motivated to change your habits for the better and help you get out of debt faster. As you pay off each debt, you'll experience a rush of pride at the freedom you experience. You will find yourself looking for small ways to save within your daily routine so that you can borrow less that month and pay back more.

By allowing yourself to stay "in the dark" about your debt situation, the problem continues to grow. You may start out not owing much but feeling a despair that keeps you from confronting the issue and leads you to expanding debt and stress. If you are looking to make more money to create a more comfortable future for yourself, the very first step is eliminating your debt so that you have the funds to invest.

Staying Out of Debt!
Avoid leveraging options that may be offered by your bank or brokerage firm. Funds may be offered to help you complete a purchase, usually 50% of the purchase value. Of course, if that stock grows and you are able to cash out at a profit, that's great. But imagine if it falls instead. Now, you've lost money and area also in debt - not just the loaned funds, but interest as well. And of course, should the stock rise, imagine how much sweeter your gains had you used only your own capital to make the purchase.

I'll invest when I'm rich.
A lot of people bring this up as their objection and defense for not investing. It is just plain silly! Saying you will wait until you are rich before you start investing is like saying:
- I will only work harder when I get promoted.
- I will cut my hair when I finally get a girlfriend.
- I promise to give it my all when I get a big break!

We all know one thing; all the promises above always work in reverse.

You only get promoted when you work hard. You get your big break when you give in your all; and finally, you will be rich only when you invest. I don't want to talk about getting a girlfriend as soon as you...

You will not land the better gig by being lazy and waiting for it, with promises of being a better employee once you do. You have to prove your worth in the role you have.

And you will not suddenly become rich without a plan to make your money work for you in the form of investment of some sort. You have to start somewhere, and for many of us, that means starting small and building from there.

Where and how do I invest?
Aside from the stock market, there are many other types of investments available. These investments include, but are not limited to bonds, time-deposits, precious metals, mutual funds, foreign currency, and many more. We will be looking at the most basic ones for now. Keep in mind that you don't have to pick just one as we go through the various investments. It is a widely known fact that successful investors do not put all their money into one investment vehicle. They diversify. But, since this is a startup guide, it would be easy to learn one at a time.

What are...?
- **Time Deposits**
  This is a fixed-deposit that cannot be withdrawn for a certain period. Generally, the higher the amount and the longer the period it is kept, the

higher the returns gained. Time deposits are useful when it comes to short term wealth. They are almost useless when it comes to wealth building. This is because their returns are always lower than inflation.

- **Bonds**

  A bond is one way an institution borrows money. You are essentially lending money to an institution when you purchase a bond. In return for lending money to the institution, you are paid interest during the life of the bond. You are also entitled to the principal amount at the end of the term.

- **Mutual Funds**

  This is a method of investing. Mutual funds are not investment vehicles of any sort. Different investors have their money pooled into a single fund. Then an investment occurs. The pooled funds could be put into bonds, equities or even foreign exchange. An expert called a "fund manager" always manages the mutual funds. The benefit here is that diversification is built-in, which reduces your risk.

- **Unit Investment Trust Funds (UITF)**

  This is similar to mutual funds in the sense that both are collective schemes that are invested and they are both managed by a fund manager. There are some technical disparities between the two, but it isn't relevant to this discussion at the moment.

- **Equities (the Stock Market)**

  A stock market is a place where you can invest in "publicly owned" or listed companies. You become a part-owner of a company by buying shares of stock of that company. You also get to participate in the company's ability to grow and make money as a part owner.

Why should I invest in the stock market?

Two reasons are categorically etched on my mind in answer to this question. The first one is purely an economic reason, while the second revolves around your growth as an investor.

1. **Higher Returns**

   Historically, the stock market has given higher average returns than bonds and inflations. Let's pick an illustration. Take a look from 20 years ago between the year 1989 and the year 2009; you will notice one thing. The performance of the stock market has outperformed bonds and savings accounts. While the growth of the stock market has been steady and peaked at 14.1% in terms of returns, bonds have a growth of 11.0% while savings accounts plus the interest paid into them have a meager 2.3%.

   It is also of high importance to stress this fact; the returns of the stock market are not guaranteed - but left over a long period, the potential for returns is great.

   Another reason to put your money into the stock market is the expert partnership. Buying the stock of a company automatically turns you into a part-owner of that corporation. It simply means that whenever the company makes money, you also make money. With a couple of dollars, you can own shares in Amazon, Royal Bank of Scotland, Everi Holdings, and many more.

Last but not least, depending on your country, your income tax at the end of the day is bearable. There are countries where money made on the stock market is not taxed while in other countries, depending on how much stock you buy, you may be taxed - albeit, a small percentage.

2. Increased Flexibility

How much money you choose to invest is up to you. Prices for shares in individual companies range from a few dollars to thousands of dollars. Most mutual funds, on the other hand, have minimums, often of $1,000 or more.

3. Financial Literacy

This is my favorite reason for encouraging investment in the stock market. You get to grow exponentially as an investor. Your responsibility increases more when you invest in the stock market than when you make a one-time bank deposit. And because of the responsibility involved, you get to learn more. There is a reward for learning more too. You get to earn more!

This is why it is important to me. I have this strong belief that financial literacy is the sole solution to poverty. We get to retain our position as the leading nation economically if every American knows how to manage their money well, how to invest, and ultimately how to create wealth.

STOCK MARKET

While the previous section focused on the "Why" questions, this section will do justice to the "What" and a bit of "How" in the stock market.

What is the stock market?

The stock market is a place where stocks of companies are publicly listed, and from where you can buy and sell shares of stock. I will elaborate on four key terms in the definition I've given:

- **A Place**: It's called a place because of the location. Unlike other countries that have just one stock exchange, The United States has 13 registered stock exchanges operating currently in the United States. But we don't have to visit all of them to trade.

- **Buy and Sell**: This is the reason it is called a stock "market." There are elected representatives who are called "Trading Participants" or brokers. These people can buy and sell stock directly. Individual investors transact with these brokers.

- **Shares of Stock**: Whether called stocks, shares of stock, or shares, they all mean the same the same thing. They represent the ownership of a company. A sole-proprietorship has just a single share which is owned by the founder of the company. However, corporations have multiple shares which can be owned by different people. These are the shares that are bought and sold in the stock market.

- **Companies that are Publicly-Listed**: The stock market does not have all registered corporations on it. Corporations must be publicly listed companies. A company that offers its shares of stock to the public is a publicly-listed company. Listing companies is usually done to put funds into expanding operations. So that the general public can invest, the company must first past strict standards set by the various stock exchanges.

In summary, the stock market is just four things:
- It is a place where (b.) you can buy and sell (c.) Shares of stock in (d.) publicly listed companies.

The stock market is made of exchanges, like the New York Stock Exchange (NYSE) and Nasdaq in the US. Exchanges bring buyers and sellers together and act as a market for the exchange of shares of the company. The exchange also tracks the supply and demand of each stock, which in turn drives the price of the stock. Stocks can't be exchanged at any time – business is conducted only during specific business hours, with some additional before- and after-hours sessions available depending on your broker.

So, how does the stock market work?
In the stock market, there are interactions between four groups. This interaction makes the stock market work. These groups are the Investors (You), the Trading Participants (Trade Brokers), The Stock Exchange, and the Publicly Listed Companies.

- **The Publicly Listed Company and the SE (Stock Exchange)**:
An application is forwarded to the Stock Exchange by the publicly listed company so they can be allowed to offer shares of stock to the public. The company is bonded to comply with very stringent requirements before the investments are opened to the public. You, as the investor, are protected by the SE. Your interests are safeguarded.
- **The SE and the Trading Participant (Broker)**: There is no direct transaction between the SE and us the investors. The only people allowed to have direct transactions are the Trading Participants. They buy and sell shares of stock. This act was enacted simply for control purposes and making work simpler. The SE makes it its priority to monitor Publicly Listed Companies while the Trading Participants deal with the investing public.
- **The Trading Participant and the Investor (You!)**: If you wish to buy or sell shares, you will have to contact a trading participant or broker. To help you do this, a broker will charge a nominal amount for fees for the buying or selling transaction. Information is also provided to you by the brokers on which companies are good to buy in addition to their transaction services.

To recap, this is how the Stock Market works: (a.) Companies who want to be publicly listed are monitored and screened by the SE. (b.) Trading Participants are assigned by the SE to interact with the public for the buying and selling of shares. (c.) Trading Participants become the middlemen between the SE and the investing public.

How do I make money in the Stock Market?

Have this in mind; investing in the stock market is buying ownership of businesses. That means you make money the same way its business owners make money. You do this through dividends and capital gains.

- **Dividends**

    Your share of earnings in the company as an investor is the dividends. If a company declares its dividends, it means one thing; they are also shareholders and are paying themselves too. That means, there is a joint partnership between you and the company. You get paid the same way they do too.

    Dividends can be paid in cash (which we then encourage you to invest into the market to capitalize your earnings further) or in additional shares paid out to shareholders in lieu of cash.

- **Capital Appreciation or Capital Gains**

    The second way to make money in the stock market is through capital appreciation. This means that the value of the company grows and is worth more than when you bought your shares.

How much money can be made in the stock market?

A percentage of the amount of money you put into the stock market is what you can gain or lose. Your willingness to learn and become disciplined in applying what you learn can affect how high or low this percentage is. Before I delve into some personal details and start calling out numbers, it is important you know that whether a percentage is high or low, it is often compared to the market average.

For instance, I had a 30% gain in the year 2011. Well, 2011 was a very good year, so I personally think this is a good average. In one of the seminars I attended, a member of the audience was asked how much money he had made in his stock trading. His answer was amazing. A hundred percent! He doubled his money in just one year. Beautiful!

This may, however, not have been the same in the year 2008 during the time of financial crisis and economic meltdowns everywhere. The average returns were negative! It means if an investor had made profit, his performance is considered above average.

Isn't the stock market risky?
It is. It is very risky. You will also be dealing with two kinds of risk: inherent risk due to market capitalization and risk due to ignorance.

- **Inherent Risk Due to Market Capitalization**
  This is a risk because you cannot, at any given time, predict the price of a stock 100%. One of the things that guide forecasting (a process of making intelligent predictions) is that a more short-term, specific prediction has a higher chance of being

wrong. The opposite is also true of this matter; the more general predictions have a higher probability to be correct.

This means that if there is a prediction that there will be an increase in the price of the stock by 10%, this week, it is very likely for it to turn out wrong when compared to a prediction that says the price of the stock would have increased by 10% over the next two years. That is why it is riskier to invest in the short term than investing for the long term. The stock market has this risky status because you cannot successfully predict the exact value of your investment. When you acknowledge that the prediction of your exact stock could be wrong, you find the amount of risk is acceptable. You can easily manage this risk by diversifying your stocks and putting in place other investment strategies.

However, when the investor assumes that his prediction may turn out correct, the inherent risk automatically becomes a huge problem. After he had settled for his prediction, the investor will be likely unprepared for the events that may unfold if he turns out wrong. This risk is a very dangerous one, and you should be aware and wary of it. The risk is due to ignorance.

- **Risk due to Ignorance**
  I have a favorite quote on investing. This quote is largely underrated though. It states that, "It's not the investment that is risky... It's the investor".

When you fully grasp this quote made by Robert Kiyosaki, you will understand that investments can have little or no risk. When the investor ends up not being able to tell the difference, the risk comes. The above quote confused me when I first read it. It took me reading it over and over again to grasp it fully. This is because it challenged one of the oldest principles in investment: "High risk, high return."

This means if Roberto Kiyosaki turns out to be right, it is possible to earn higher returns, without having to take on higher risks. You only need to become a smarter investor. This is both confusing and empowering at the same time. Upon further study, I fell across this passage from the book *The Intelligent Investor*.

"It has been an old and sound principle that those who cannot afford to take risks should be content with a relatively low return on their invested funds. From this, there has developed the general notion that the rate of return with which the investor should aim for is more or less proportionate to the degree of risk he is ready to run. Our view is different. **The rate of return sought should be dependent, rather on the amount of intelligent effort the investor is willing and able to bring to bear on his task. The minimum returns go to our passive investor, who wants both safety and freedom from concern. The maximum return would be realized by the alert and enterprising**

investor who exercises maximum intelligence and skill."

Benjamin Graham *(The Intelligent Investor)*

Reading this, especially the text emboldened, made me feel great. I felt great because I realized that there is no dependency on the success in the stock market on chance. It depended on disciplined study rather.

Overall, the risks of investing in the stock market is dramatized. There are some people who suffer big losses with severe consequences. However, the majority of investors have found safe strategies that reduce the risks. As with all subjects, the media reports only the extremes in market fluctuation.

Keep in mind that investments in the stock market are meant to be long-term. One financial expert, Dave Ramsey, says, "The only people who get hurt riding a roller coaster are the ones that jump off." Simply put, if you panic and sell off when there is a temporary drop in the price of your stocks, you face the biggest risk. You have to keep in mind the long-term.

Understand Your Risk Tolerance

We all vary in our tolerance to risk. This tolerance is influenced by genetics, education, income, wealth, and age and refers to how much you can psychologically stand to risk. Risk tolerance is also affected by our perception of how risky an action is. For some, riding on an airplane may be perceived as having a high risk, while for others, riding the subway may incite more anxiety. Finances can be very personal for some of us and can create very strong emotional responses. It is important to know what your limits are in terms of how much you can invest and the types of risks you are able to tolerate so that you don't set yourself up a stress-filled investment experience.

How much money do I put in the stock market?

As an average investor, the money you should put into the stock market is money that you won't need today, tomorrow, next year, or in five or even ten years. The reason is this; you cannot and can never exactly predict the value that your investment will turn out to hold in the coming years. So, even as I stated earlier that the average return the stock market had from 1989 to 2009 was 14% per year, future returns are never exactly guaranteed.

It is also recommended that you don't purchase all of your stock at once. If you're planning a purchase, split this up into three amounts and purchase shares 30 days apart. This way, you reduce some of your risk and build confidence in your abilities to choose the best companies to invest in.

The Biggest Problem with Investing

I don't know how this may sound to you, but I will say it anyway. The biggest problem that can spring up in investment is when some personal problems or challenges of yours force you to suddenly sell off your investments for cash when the market is down.

Let's take the story of Danny, for example. He invested all of his savings – reaching up to $5600 in the stock market. He hoped that someday, the money would serve as a down payment for a house. Unfortunately, there was an accident. The bones in his left leg were crushed. To get his legs fixed and on the road to total recovery would cause him around $5600. Even though the company Danny works for offers benefits for medical incidences, his employer could only pay $1000. That leaves Danny to find a way to pay for his share of the treatment which amounts to $4600. The stock market is the only place Danny had money. Unluckily, it was a down market, and the value of his investment was just $4600.

This didn't surprise Danny one bit. It had happened in the past. The value of stocks would plunge down and then it would shoot up again. Normally, Danny waited it out. But not this time. He just couldn't afford to wait for the values to climb up again before paying his hospital bills. So, he went ahead and withdrew his investment worth $4600 - which is taking a loss of $1000.

This is one among the list of discouraging things that can happen when you put all your money in the stock market.

Make sure this doesn't happen to you!
You can use one of the three ways I will list below to prevent the problem above and protect your investment

whenever there is a sudden need for cash. Before you invest in the stock market, I strongly recommend that you do all of them.

- **Be Insured:**
  Yes, get insurance that will cover you in the case of accidents (it could be you in it, your loved ones, your car, your home or your business). The insurance company will be obligated to pay for damages, and at the same time, there would be no need for taking money out of your investments to fix things.

- **Keep aside an emergency fund**:
  Emergency funds are sums of money kept aside in the case of an emergency. The cash that should be kept aside should total six months of your total yearly living expenses. There may be incidences in your life which are unplanned or won't be covered by insurance. For example, if you lose your job, there are funds to survive on before the next job comes along.

- **Remember to only put in money you won't need for a very long time:** For you to be able to do that, you have to have a very good grasp of the amount you will be spend. And remember to always remove the once-a-year expenses like birthdays and holidays. You may find it tempting to touch your investments if the 13th-month salary isn't enough for your Christmas expenses.

Investing in the stock market is a marathon, not a sprint!

I can't emphasize this enough! ONLY INVEST MONEY YOU WON'T NEED for several years. Longevity of investment is where the money is made. If you are constantly investing and then cashing out when you find yourself low on readily-available funds to meet your immediate needs, you will be in a constant state of stress. You will also continuously lose money if you're withdrawing money at inopportune times. It can be difficult to determine a good balance between setting money aside in investment for the future and ensuring you have all that you need while you wait for it to grow. Developing a detailed budget will be helpful here.

How much time do I need to spend doing it?

This is wholly dependent on you and your investment strategy. Some people go through their portfolio once in a while in such a way that if the total time is calculated, it amounts to one hour per year. Others check it so frequently that it sums up to up to eight hours per day! Now that is a bit much.

When one of my friends started, he always took the time to look at his portfolio every hour. It was exciting to him watching and seeing how his money went up and horrifying to see the same thing go down. He kept checking it out even though he didn't "do" anything with it. His habit only lasted for about two weeks before he got used to it. Now, seeing his money on either +15% or -15% doesn't matter much to him anymore. He came to realize

164

that checking it frequently is boring and, well, a waste of time.

What does he do now? He just spends up to twenty or thirty minutes every other Saturday or Sunday to read up his stocks. And at the end of every month, he spends a little more time to place his buy orders in the stock market. He spends more time studying the stock market now than simply gawking at the figures at his portfolio and illogically cheering it on.

Do you know what my friend's story shows? It is this: there is little or no relationship between the amount of time spent "buying and selling' and the amount you can make in the stock market. Instead, the amount of money you will make is proportional to how much the quality of what you have learned is being applied.

The Millionaire Next Door is a bestselling book by Thomas Stanley, Ph.D. and William Danko. The book studied the lifestyles of the wealthiest men in America. Over 500 millionaires and over 11,000 high-net-worth and high-income individuals were interviewed by the duo. Questions asked about ranged from their cars, suits, shoes, vacations, houses, worries, and much more. And most importantly, they asked about how long they kept investments in a specific company. This is what they found out:

a. **90% of millionaire investors are not active traders in the market:**

A great number of them hold their stocks for a minimum of one year. An even higher number of the majority holds their stock for a minimum of 6 years or more.

b. **Billionaires take their time to study far fewer offerings (companies):**
   This has made it possible for them to focus their time and energy to master their comprehension of a much smaller variety of offerings in the market.

We suggest not being overly active in trading. Remember, this is a marathon, not a sprint. Stock market investments are meant to be long-term. You by no means need to check on your stocks daily. Checking them quarterly, when you receive your reports, is plenty. Daily review increases your stress level and may keep you focused on the share price rather than the value of the company, which of course is the most important.

Do I have to have millions already before I can start investing?

The answer is no! With extensive use of the internet, you can start investing for as low as $100. The major limitation of the past was that you needed a stockbroker that is personal to you to be able to invest. So a minimum amount of investments were set by the stockbrokers who had limited time before they accepted individual investors. But today, there are stockbrokers online who allow you to invest in the stock market on your own and in your way. All that is needed is a computer and an internet connection that is stable. It is that easy as you can send your buy or sell orders online. The minimum starting amount is much lower because you don't go through the hassle of meeting and talking with a live person.

Here are websites where you can find some of these online brokers. It is expedient to have it in mind that this list is not complete.

Online Stock Brokers
BPI Securities Corporation - www.bpitrade.com
Merrill Edge - www.merrilledge.com
E Trade - www.us.etrade.com
TD Ameritrade - www.tdameritrade.com
COL Financial Inc. - www.colfinancial.com
First Metro Securities Brokerage Corporation - www.firstmetrosec.com.ph

I make use of **CitisecOnline**. No one is paying me to promote them. Being a satisfied customer, I highly recommend them. They have one of the largest online brokerages in the world. They are also one of the very active ones when it comes to promoting stock market education. Introductory stock market seminars are held every week at their office. That's to show you how customer-focused they are.

Won't this be stressful?
There is a high relation between stress and risk. One cannot do without the other. (See the answer to 'Isn't the stock market risky?'). A risky investor is a stressed investor. Stress comes as a result of the feeling of being out of control, and not knowing what next to do. And not

knowing what to do next is simply caused by a lack of information. This is caused by a lack of research.

Imagine the scenario of two college students taking a Calculus exam. Student 1 studied several weeks before the exam. Student 2 just started studying the night before. Who do you think would have to deal with more stress before, during, and after the exam?

Now let's turn the example around and use it in the stock market. Josh just heard the news that his officemate, Jake just made $1200 in one day from the stock market. He went ahead and asked a friend for more information. This will let him in on the next big thing on the stock market. A couple of days later his friend tells Josh to put his investment in ABC Company so that could double his money in a week. Josh gets excited over the news, and on the same day, invests his $3000 savings into ABC.

Josh looks at his account the next day and what is left of his money is just $2,800. He turns to his friend and demands an explanation from him. His friend laughs at him and explains in few words that it will recover and that it's a natural phenomenon that occurs. His friend advises Josh to take a look at his account in a week when it's already doubled. Josh being very trusting follows the advice. A week later, he goes back to his account.... And zap! Account Balance: $300. That is 90% of his savings gone like that in one week.

Just think about the stress Josh was going through. He put all of the blame on his friend for losing his money and promised that he would never put his money as an investment in the stock market again. Josh was unprepared and took on a lot of risk due to ignorance. Now, we all know he won't be able to sleep at night because of the stress.

So prepare very well if you don't want the stress. It's that simple.

I am not smart enough! It is just too complicated!

It's just new. It's not complicated, so take it one step at a time. A lot of people think that it is complicated, and because I already know it, I think it's easy. So to see if it's complicated, I ran a little experiment.

I clicked and logged on to my online account, and ran through all the terms a 5th grader probably won't understand. I also went ahead and counted the number of click you had to make for the basic transactions. Then, I discovered that, of the 90 new terms which will be shown to you when you start investing, you'll only have to remember 32 of them. The rest of the terms aren't really important. This is just like the buttons in your TV/DVD remote. Count the number of buttons available in your TV remote, and then count how many of those buttons you use. Our TV remote has 49 buttons, but I just use 5 of those buttons: Power, Channel Up, Channel Down, Volume Up and Volume Down. If I show our TV remote to a person who has never seen one before, I'm sure they'll also say it's very complicated.

After you finish reading this guide, you'll be able to understand all of those 32 terms, plus a little bit more.

And once you buy your first stock, you'll realize how simple it is, what you see when you open the order window. What's important for your first buy?

GETTING STARTED

How do I start investing in the stock market?

There are three ways to get your money into the stock market. The key here is to find which best fits your desired style of investing.

a. **Through a Mutual Fund (Equity Funds)**
   A Mutual Fund is a type of investment wherein the money is pooled from many investors. These funds are professionally handled by the fund manager. Since there are several types of mutual funds, what you should look for is an "Equity Fund," or a fund that has a percentage of it invested in the stock market.

   In a mutual fund, you are not buying a specific company. Instead, what you are buying are shares of that specific fund. So if the fund is invested in 10 different companies, your money is also invested in those ten different companies. This also means that you no longer have to decide which companies' stocks to buy and when to sell them. That responsibility is delegated to the fund manager. So if convenience is what you're after, an equity mutual fund may be for you.

b. Through a Traditional Stockbroker

A traditional stockbroker is a living, breathing person who is licensed to give you professional advice on your investments. The good thing about this is that you can get counsel specifically tailored to your investing needs, your investment goals, your timeline, and your tolerance to risk. A good stock broker will be able to advise you on what to buy and when to sell - and notify you of the upcoming opportunities. You can even assign some brokers to manage your portfolio for you while you go on vacation.

The many personalized services that come with this method entail a price – commonly in the form of higher commission rates and higher minimums for starting an account.

c. Through an Online Stock Broker

Investing through an online stockbroker is like being your own stockbroker. On your own, you will be able to buy and sell stocks as long as you have a computer with access to the Internet. Since everything is do-it-yourself, you will be paying the lowest commission rate possible (0.25%).

As for market tips and advice, your online broker would be providing you with tons of reports and market information. It would be up to you how to understand it and how to get the relevant details.

COL Financial, the online broker that I'm using, even created a short-list of companies which they highly recommend to their clients. They call it the Easy-Investment-Program or EIP. I'll talk about this later.

Which among the three options should I choose?
Among these three options, what I generally recommend to starting investors is to start with an online stock broker. Here are the reasons why:
- The minimum amount to start is just $15. This makes it accessible to almost anyone who has a steady source of income. New investors most likely haven't amassed the wealth required to get a full-service broker.
- You're on your own. You will read the company reports. You will decide which companies to buy, and which companies to sell. You will execute your buy and sell orders. You will manage your portfolio. This means you stand to earn the biggest amount. And because you're the one doing everything, you get the biggest advantage.
- You learn everything. This is the number-one reason why I would recommend doing it on your own first, before getting a mutual fund. In a mutual fund, everything is managed for you. Your only responsibility is to write a check or make a deposit to the mutual fund company. (Developing the skill of writing a check and paying someone is

very dangerous!). In effect, you're putting up all the capital, but taking none of the responsibility. From a business perspective, that's very risky.

I hope you don't misunderstand. I'm not saying that you shouldn't invest in mutual funds. I also have investments in mutual funds. But if you want to become a good investor, you'll learn much faster when you're doing it on your own.

How do I pick a stockbroker?
A couple of things you should consider when selecting a stockbroker are the following:
- **Broker's Fees**:
  For every transaction you make, the broker will get a certain percentage of that amount. The lowest that is allowable by the PSE is 0.25% of the transaction value. There are other fees which are mandatory such as VAT, PSE Transaction Fees, SCCP, and Sales Tax. These other fees, however, would not vary from broker to broker.
- **Market Information Available:**
  The professional (non-generic) information and advice provided to you is the justification for why brokers charge higher than 0.25%. This is why with online brokers (where only generic market information is provided), they charge the minimum.
- **Trust, Reputation, and Stability:**
  It is very important that you ensure your broker is registered with the Philippine Stock Exchange and is not a scam. Here is a complete list of online and

traditional brokers registered with the PSE. (Broker Directory). A ranking report by volume of transactions is also available in that link.

- **DRIPs (Dividend Reinvestment Programs)**

Some brokers offer programs that automatically take the dividends   paid to you and reinvest them by purchasing more shares of that   stock for you. If you let this run over time, you can have significantly   greater earnings as the dividends will capitalize over time.

Overall, you should pick a broker who matches your investing needs. As a beginning investor with little starting capital, it would be best to pick brokers with the lowest fees. This way, more of your available money is put into stocks rather than transaction fees.

Take the Leap - Quick Tip!

There's no need to waste time picking and researching brokers. Just choose CitisecOnline (COLFinancial.com). They have the lowest fees. It's very easy to invest with them, and they provide a lot of market information. They are one of the largest online brokerage in the world, offering you a higher level of stability in the investment community.

Another option is Ally (formerly TradeKing). There is no minimum initial deposit to open an investment account. And the site offers low fees for purchasing stocks. They are ranked number one on comparebroker.com among accounts with no minimums.

INVESTMENT STRATEGIES

In this section, you'll learn about the different options you have for investing in the stock market. Some are simple, while some are a little more complicated. Take a look at which one would be best for you.

What are the common investing methods?

There are three basic methods of investing: (1) Buy and Hold, (2) Dollar Cost Averaging and (3) Market Timing (or trading). Here you'll learn about each one and why it works.

1. **Buy and Hold**

    The buy and hold strategy is buying a stock and holding onto it until the end of time (meaning, until you want/need to get the money). This strategy is relatively stress-free since you'll be ignoring the daily/weekly/monthly ups and downs of the market. This can be done when you have a sum of money that you don't need now or later in the future – but you just want it off your hands. The important thing here is that you're not attached to the money. If it gets bigger, great! But if it gets lost, then you should still be okay.

    With a buy and hold strategy, it's best to pick the giants of today's industry. Pick the companies that will most probably outlive you. These are the companies that have a history of expanding into new ways of making money. Here are some examples:

- PLDT, the leading Philippines network provider, used to be known only as a provider of telephone services. Then they expanded their business to also provide internet and cellular services. Much more recently, they even acquired a competitor, Sun Cellular.
- Jollibee Foods Corporation, also in the Philippines, began by just selling Ice Cream. Then the business shifted to selling hot dogs. After the hotdogs, came the Yumburgers and Chickenjoy. When they couldn't sell any more chicken, they bought Greenwich. This marked their entrance in the pizza-pasta business. Now they own Chowking, Red Ribbon, and Burger King Philippines. And I'm sure you've heard the news that they purchased Mang Inasal.
- San Miguel Corporation, in the Philippines has been recognized for its world-famous San Miguel Beer. But aside from this product, SMC has had a history of expanding into new businesses. Some of these businesses are Meralco, Philippine Airlines and Petron Corporation. San Miguel Corporation will keep on evolving to thrive in the ever-changing market.

A Word of Caution: There is no guarantee that investing in these same

companies today will yield the same returns 11 years from now. If it was the year 2009 – and you had put your money in San Miguel Corporation, your returns would have been negative in 2012.

2. Dollar Cost Averaging

The dollar cost averaging method is a simple, safe, and effective way to make money in the stock market. However, it requires more discipline than the buy and hold strategy. The dollar cost averaging strategy is investing a fixed amount of money in a good company at fixed intervals, regardless of its price. This way, you spread out the risk of buying at high prices, and at the same time take advantage of the opportunities at low prices.

Dollar Cost Averaging is discussed at length in Benjamin Graham's book, *The Intelligent Investor*, which Warren Buffett called "by the far the best book on investing ever written." It has been a guide many successful investors have trusted for years.

Because you're able to purchase more shares when the price is low, the weight of the lower prices is greater. As a result, the average purchase price also goes lower. This is the magic of dollar cost averaging. By buying at fixed intervals, with fixed amounts of money, you take advantage of the price fluctuations. Because you are always invested, you will not be devastated by the losses inherent in trying to time the market, which can be difficult.

Say, for example, you are buying $500 every month in stock using this strategy. The first month, the stock price is $10. You're able to buy 50 shares. The next month, the stock price is $5. Rather than becoming upset and looking for an exit strategy that might leave you with a 50% loss, you instead revel in the ability to buy 100 shares. You'll now have 150 shares in a company whose stock price will likely rise once again. Plus, you've saved yourself a great deal of stress by trusting in a strategy designed by investment giants.

3. Market Timing

Market timing is also known as stock trading. This means actively watching the stock market for opportunities to buy at the lows and sell at the highs. Market timing requires more skill, time and dedication. At the same time, it is also a lot more exciting.

If you're willing to check on the stock market daily, and you want the excitement, this may be for you. With timing the market, you can double your money in a week! But at the same time, the reverse could happen. You could also lose half your money in that same week if you're not careful. This rush of winning and losing is the reason that the stock market is often likened to gambling.

While the concept of buying at the lows and selling at the highs seem simple, it requires knowledge of a science called technical analysis. Technical analysis is a technique where you observe patterns in the stock charts and look for different market indicators. You also can fall victim to bad advice from "investment psychics," and experience more overall stress from attempting to track your investments through the ups and downs and rushing to buy and sell at "just the right times."

Take the Leap - Quick Tip!
Of these three strategies, the best strategy for the new investor is peso cost
averaging. You don't need to have huge amounts of capital. You spread your risk. You only need to check on it once or twice a month. It's best for a long-term investment.

If you already have a huge amount of money set-aside (say, P100, 000 and above), divide that portion into 6 portions (or so) and slowly invest it into the stock market using the peso-cost averaging.

CAN SLIM Investing System
There are as many investment strategies as there are investors. One that has worked well for many is the CAN SLIM system. CAN SLIM serves as an acronym for a set of rules to follow.

Current Quarterly Earnings - Watch for stocks that are showing increases in their quarterly earnings of 25% or more.

Annual Earnings Growth - Great companies show growth in annual earnings of at least 25% for at least three years.

New Product, Service, Management, or Price High - Most of the companies who are performing best have something new to offer that consumers can't find anywhere else. Think of the incredible booms Apple experienced upon release of the original iPhone and iPad. These products were limited and pushed the limits of technology. Technological advances are often great investment opportunities.

Supply and Demand - When shares are limited, prices increase. The concept of supply and demand in stock broking is consistent with those in consumer economics in general.

Leader or Laggard - Buy from those who are leading the way in their respective industries. You'll be able to expect innovation and building stock values.

Institutional Sponsorship - Follow the moves of the professional investors managing large portfolios, like mutual funds and pension funds. These investments make up 75% of market activity. Observing closely the choices made by professionals will benefit your own personal portfolio.

Market Direction - Studies show that 3 of four stocks follow the trend of the market at large, so tracking trends will lead you to making the best investment choices.

How do I know which companies to invest in?

The first thing to keep in mind when choosing which companies to invest in is that you're buying a share of the company - which means you're becoming a part owner. So, you need to look at the business as a whole. Don't just focus on the symbols on the ticker. Think of the company. Is this a company you want to be a part-owner of? This is the number-one question to consider.

Why is this a company you're committed to? Keep that in mind - and write it down to review when you're feeling particularly panicky. Think ahead about what might cause you to sell the stocks. When you think about dissolving the investment, look back at those reasons. Is it time to let go, or are you acting rashly?

Professionals use two approaches in deciding which companies to buy stock in: fundamental analysis and technical analysis. Before I explain these two methods, please be reminded that the people who do it are professionals, meaning they spend the majority of their workweek performing these kinds of analyses.

Now, rest assured that you do not need to learn how to do this. I'm just discussing it here so that you have an idea of how it's done. (In the next section, I'll be sharing with you a very practical and convenient way of investing wherein you can leverage on the expertise of these professionals.)

Fundamental Analysis

Fundamental analysis is a technique that estimates the potential value of a stock by focusing on underlying factors that affect a company's business and its future growth. The approach is usually made in a top-down manner, from general to specific. The following example I'll be giving is extremely broad. Don't get scared or overwhelmed, since you don't need to do this. I'm just sharing it so you understand the depth of this technique. The following list is the series of questions one would need to answer using the fundamental analysis approach on a global level.

• Which region is growing? Europe? North America? Asia?
• Which countries in that region have the highest potential for growth?
• Which industries in that country drive the growth?
• Which companies are the leaders in those industries?
• Will these companies continue to be leaders in their industries?

Again, don't worry, because you don't need to do this when you start investing. When I was just starting to study how to invest in the stock market, this was one of the first things that I read; and it overwhelmed me! I felt like I had to read my book from Econ 101 again! (I was supposed to say
"Econ 101 notes" but then I remembered that I didn't take down notes when I was in college!)

Fundamental Analysis: Simpler Version

To make fundamental analysis easier, the best first step is to start with what you already know. Start by identifying the products that you already use and find out who makes them. You'll be surprised that the makers of those products and services are listed in the stock market.

Which fast food restaurants do you eat in? - Take a look and see if it's owned by TriCorp.

Do you use natural gas? (Of course, you do) - Find out more about Consumer's Energy.

Do you have cable or Internet service? - Look into AT&T or Comcast.

Where do you shop? (Likely the company is listed on the stock market.)

What banks do you go to? Which airlines do you use for travel? Where do you work? If you closely take a look at all of the things you use, you'll have multiple companies with which you can start your research.

A good rule of thumb is to invest in companies that you are familiar with. Think of those companies that came to mind above. You know the products and services they offer. You know how relatively successful they are. All of these things create additional confidence as you invest.

For each of these companies, your goal is to find evidence that these companies will continue to grow in the future. If you can't find any evidence, then don't put your money in it. The more evidence you have, the better your chance of making a good choice.

Which can convince you to buy a stock?
The following list contains examples of "evidence" which you could encounter when studying these companies. As you go through the list, you'll observe that there are pieces of evidence which you'll find ridiculous. I've put them there because there are people who buy stocks based on it. Also, you'll find these ridiculous statements slowly turn into possibly reasonable ones with a few changes.

Which are good enough reasons for you to buy a stock?
- The market share of company XYZ's major product A increased by 10%.
- The net profit of Company XYZ increased by 10% this year.
- Company XYZ's net profit has been growing consistently for the past ten years.
- A guy on the road who was randomly interviewed on TV said, "There are too many condos here in Metro Manila! I don't even know anyone who buys them."
- A guy on the road, dressed in a suit who was randomly interviewed on TV said, "I can afford those condos. But I've never considered buying them."

184

- A professor of economics who was being interviewed on TV said, "There are already too many condos in Metro Manila. I don't know why these developers are still building them."
- A representative of Ayala during an interview said, "Our research shows that there is a lot of demand for condominiums. Come 2015, all these units would be sold out. So it would be best to buy them now as they're pre-selling at a discounted price."
- My boss just invested $10 million into company XYZ!
- My boss, who is well connected with other investors just invested in company XYZ!
- My boss, whose wife is a mutual fund manager of an international bank, just invested P10m into company XYZ!

As you do your research, you'll be able to uncover a lot of information. Some will make sense while others won't. Some evidence will be based on ten years of performance, while some will be based on the latest rumors. In the end, it will be up to you to decide - because it's your money that will be at stake.

Different Types of Investment:
- **Growth investing** takes advantage of new medical breakthroughs or technologies released by strong companies. You leave room for growth and these investments tend to have a high profit to earnings ratio.
- **Value investing** involves buying stock in companies who have been on a downturn but can

be turned around with better management to become a more profitable company. This takes a little faith and a little knowledge of business potential.

- **ProActive Investing** is a combination of the two types above, using options to reduce the cost of the purchase and create revenue during the dreaded wait-time.

Technical Analysis

Technical Analysis is a technique which estimates the future value of a stock by reviewing historical price charts and patterns. The major assumption in technical analysis is that everything that has happened and is happening is already factored into the stock price. And therefore, by studying the stock price alone, you have already factored in everything that could affect the price including fundamental factors and the market psychology.

In short, you only consider the price of the stock with technical analysis. This is in contrast with fundamental analysis where everything seems like a factor to consider. This makes technical analysis look a lot simpler, making more people want to try it out. The dangerous thing is that it's not that simple and it would take more than reading a few articles on the Internet to learn this skill. The seminars on this (offered by CitisecOnline) have two sessions, each one going for at least 4 hours.

I have decided to end the discussion on technical analysis here. The reason is that I do not want to encourage you to try it without more in-depth training. At this point, it is enough that you know that Technical Analysis exists. Now, if you want to learn more, I've provided references in the last section of this guide.

Fundamental and technical analysis seem like a lot of work! Is there another way?
Yes, there is a better, easier, safer, and more effective way to do it!

It's to learn from experts. Isaac Newton, one of the most influential scientists of all time said, "If I have seen further, it is by standing on the shoulders of giants." So, even though you're new to the stock market, if you look up and follow the experts, you can get good returns in the stock market. At the same time, you will be able to learn a lot because you're still the one responsible for managing your money.

I call this method "Practical Investing." And I love it because it's the way the majority of people (especially those who don't have time) can safely and profitably invest in the Stock Market.

PRACTICAL INVESTING
Practical Investing is a method of investing wherein you simply follow a stock recommendation list given by experts in the Stock Market. This way you get to leverage their time and talent when it comes to choosing stocks.

Who are these experts that can guide me in my investing?

There are a lot of sources online wherein you can get this guidance. A few are great, some are okay, and many are just plain risky. So to answer this question, I will just recommend the best one. I believe that this expert is the best because of the consistency, reliability, integrity, and ease of use.

The Best Source: Bo Sanchez's Stocks Update

Bo Sanchez is the author of the best-selling book, *My Maid Invests in the Stock Market*. Bo Sanchez taught his maids and drivers how to invest in the stock market. The latest news that I read was that his maid already had P100, 000+ in her portfolio. (Yes, he's that good at teaching the stock market.) Bo's motto was that if he could teach his maids how to invest in the stock market, he could teach it to anyone! So, when he already mastered making the stock market simple and easy, he created the "StocksUpdate."

The Stocks Update is a 5-7 page article which contains stock recommendations and the reasons why that company is being recommended. The best part is that it answers the four most important questions you'll have as a stock market investor:

- What company should I buy?
- At what price should I buy it?
- When should I sell it?

Learn and Earn at the Same Time

By the way, did you notice that I said there were four questions, but only gave you 3? Well, here's the last one. The last and most important question that should be asked by an investor is:

- **Why**?

In the StocksUpdate, the "why" is answered by providing you updates on those recommended companies. You get to learn about the company's net income, expansion plans, growth targets, assets and liabilities, and other relevant financial information.

How were the recommendations in the StocksUpdate made?

It's a combination of fundamental as well as some technical analysis. The specific steps, however, are not publicly available. However, this stock recommendation list is considered to be best because of the minds that created it.

The Stocks Update Mastermind

The "mastermind" of the StocksUpdate is not Bo Sanchez, but his good friend and mentor Edward Lee. Edward Lee is not that popular to the average Filipino, but in the world of the stock market, he's a giant.

Edward was introduced to the stock market at the very young age of 18. And at that time, he was fascinated by it and even borrowed other people's money to invest in it. One year later, the stock market crashed, and he was completely wiped out. He was even buried in debt because he used borrowed money for investing!

But, thankfully for all of us, that stock market crash taught him a lesson. He persevered, recovered, and continued studying and investing in the stock market. Today (35+ years later), he is a stock market giant. He's the founder of COLFinancial, the online broker that I'm recommending to you; and he is also a self-made billionaire! (Yes, with a B!)

Standing on the Shoulders of 2 Giants

The best way to look at the StocksUpdate, then, is to see it as a product of 2 giants: Edward Lee, the stock market genius, and Bo Sanchez, the brilliant and inspiring motivational speaker.

Edward Lee provides the technical expertise of the recommendations. Then, Bo Sanchez translates the recommendations into a simple and entertaining manner in the StocksUpdate.

How do I get a copy of the StocksUpdate?

The StocksUpdate is a benefit of being a member of the Truly Rich Club. The Truly Rich Club is an online group created by Bo Sanchez. It's called "Truly Rich" because the members are taught not only to be financially wealthy, but also how to be blessed in the areas of life: relationships, career, spirituality, health, and of course finances.

Bo believed that being rich is useless if you're not healthy, or if you don't have the energy to enjoy your money. Having a lot of money will also be useless if you don't have people to enjoy it with!

That's why he takes on a very holistic and practical approach to achieving financial abundance in the Truly Rich Club.

As a member, you get e-books, recordings of live seminars, and financial newsletters aside from the StocksUpdate. Now, I'll just give a quick run through of the things you'll get as a Truly Rich Club member because I believe that this is the best guidance you can get as you start investing.

The Truly Rich Club Member Benefits
In the following table, I've outlined what you'll get as a member, including the StocksUpdate.

Benefit
1. **StocksUpdate:** Your ultimate step-by-step guide to investing in the stock market (as shown in the previous sections).

2. **Power Talks:** These are the best of Bo's seminar recordings every month. These are inspirational and transformative talks that will teach you how to live the life that want. (Sent twice a month)

3. **Success Mentors Collection:** These are interview recordings of Bo with his mentor's like Edward Lee (stock market), Larry Gamboa (real estate), and many others. Through these interviews, you get to learn not only from Bo, but other experts as well. (Sent quarterly)

4. **Wealth Strategies:** This is a newsletter that gives you financial education. Topics range from the principles of abundance to the nitty-gritty details of business, insurance and other investments.

Bonus: Free Learning Materials!

These are the one-time bonuses that you'll receive when you sign-up:
- Audio: How to be Truly Rich Seminar
- E-book: How to Turn Thoughts into Things
- E-book: How to Conquer Your Goliaths

Bonus: Earn Online as an Affiliate
As a member of the Truly Rich Club, you're also given the opportunity to earn online. If you share the Truly Rich Club with friends and family (and they sign-up) using your link, you will get to earn a commission. This is just to give the members a taste of "passive income".

Please take note that this is only a bonus and it's purely optional.

100% Transparency Disclaimer: Since I am a member of the Truly Rich Club, I have the bonus opportunity to earn some income from it. So when you sign up using my link, I will get a commission from your subscription. However, income aside, my recommendation is always based on my personal experience that the product provides excellent and valuable service.

Stock Market for Pinoys Affiliate Bonus: Now, since I'll be earning a small amount of money when you join the Truly Rich Club using my link (visit www.StockMarketforPinoys.com/trc/begin), I'd like to give you additional bonuses when you sign-up, just as a thank you.

The Membership Cost

Membership to the Truly Rich Club is not free. I am currently paying P497 per month (roughly P17/day) to get these benefits. There are also other membership options which have different prices and benefits. The details need not be discussed here. However, what I think you'll find interesting is that there's a "30-day 'no-questions-asked' money back guarantee". This means you can try out the membership, get 100% access to the materials, and then if you don't like it, just ask for a refund. They will give your money back, with no questions asked. So, there's absolutely no risk to just try it out.

Interesting... So it's okay that I just follow the Truly Rich Club list?

You have to read this section first. You see, the only time following a stock recommendation list would be irresponsible is if you act on it blindly, without knowing the source and its credibility. Let me explain using this story:

There was a young and beautiful girl, who lived in a hut by the ocean, named Marimar. Her evil aunt, named

Angelica, told Marimar that her husband Sergio has been cheating on her.

Being very gullible, Marimar believed Angelica and went home crying to seek comfort from her dog, Polgoso. Marimar was so angry and hopeless (and irresponsible) that she packed her things and left the country without saying goodbye to anyone. During the trip, she got into an accident and died.

Now, Marimar failed to do something that she should have done after she got the information. She should have first checked the credibility of two things: the credibility of the source of information and the credibility of the information itself.

(For the benefit of the very young readers, the above story is just a reference to the 1994 Telenovela entitled Marimar. It was a show that swept the Philippine TV during its time. I still have the introductory song memorized! Oh, and the story above wasn't the real plot of the show.)

Anyway, whenever you're following a stock recommendation list, it is a must to know the credibility of the source and the reliability of the information. You need to ask:

- Who is the person making the recommendation? (Source Credibility)
- How well have these recommendations been performing? (Information Credibility)

Truly Rich Club Credibility

The founder of the Truly Rich Club is Bo Sanchez. He is a spiritual preacher, best-selling author, publisher, international speaker, entrepreneur, millionaire, philanthropist, father, and husband. He has built many ministries for the poor and less fortunate; he has achieved many awards, and the list of his accomplishments is just too many to mention here.

Now, I'd like to make something clear here: Bo Sanchez is not a stock market expert. If he were the one doing the analysis, I wouldn't be so comfortable following the recommendations. However, I'm a strong believer in the Truly Rich Club recommendations because of Bo's mentor and partner in the stock market, Edward Lee.

Edward Lee is known as the "Warren Buffet" of the Philippines. He is a self-made billionaire and the chairman and founder of CitisecOnline. He started investing in the stock market when he was only 18 years old. Today, he has almost 40 years of experience under his belt. It is because of Edward Lee that the credibility of the Truly Rich Club is unrivaled.

Under the guidance of Edward Lee, the Truly Rich Club has been recommending stocks for the past two years. And so far, the performance has been stellar.

I encourage you to join the Truly Rich Club as you start investing in the stock market. It's the best guidance out there, and you get a complete package for your financial education.

Take the Leap - Quick Tip!

Join the Truly Rich Club. With the StocksUpdate newsletter, it would be like having an expert babysitter for your investing. You'll know exactly: (1) What companies to buy, (2) When exactly to buy them, (3) At what prices to buy them, and (4) When to sell them.

Important: When you sign up, remember to sign up through any of the links in this book, or on the stockmarketforpinoys.com website. That way, I'll be able to give you exclusive bonuses and step-by-step tutorials on how to invest the Truly Rich Club Way.

Truly Rich Club Links
1.   Signing up and Getting the Stock Market for Pinoys.com Bonuses
2. Truly Rich Club More Information Page
3.   Performance Review of the StocksUpdate Recommendations
4. Video Tour of the Truly Rich Club

Thank you and I hope you enjoy this audiobook, the only thing is I ask is if you could please leave a review after listening.

SECTION 2: STOCK MARKET – EXPLORING TO THE FULLEST

This part is purely optional. However, it is suggested that you still read it. I've only included this part for people who are more curious than the rest. So, there are many investors who have no clue about the topics listed below, and it doesn't hurt them (even if they don't know it). But of course, the more you know, the better, right?

On Initial Public Offerings (IPO)

What is an IPO?
An IPO is short for 'Initial Public Offering.' This refers to the first time the public is given an opportunity to buy shares of a new, publicly-listed company. Of course, this happens after PSE screens the company to protect the investing public.

IPOs are very exciting since they may present an opportunity to make a lot of money. The investing public is a bit biased towards IPOs. People remember, retell, and exaggerate the money they made on the successful ones, while the IPOs that failed or performed less than spectacular are quickly forgotten or castigated (you may have read a lot of stories about Facebook's IPO on the internet).

Here are three IPO examples and their stories:

PureGold's opening day was a bad day. Its opening price was P12.50, but it closed at P11.00. If you sold your shares immediately on that day, you would have already lost 12% of your money. However, for those who stuck with it for the next couple of months, they would have nearly doubled their money.

East West Bank's IPO opening day seemed like a good start since its price shot up to P19.78 from P18.50. However, you'll see that the excitement quickly died down in the following days.

The IPO of **Cebu Pacific** was also well received on its opening day. News also said that it was "oversubscribed." This meant that a lot of people wanted to buy the stock. It climbed from P125 to P133 on its first day. However, after several months, the stock price gradually declined. Many people held on to the stock believing that it would one day get back up again. One year passed, but sadly the stock price dropped even more. (In July 2012, the stock price was only in the P67 - P70 range.

How do I get into an IPO?
The first person to go to if you want to get into an IPO is your stockbroker. If you have an online broker and don't see any notifications on your home screen, then it would be best to call them.

As soon as you hear the news of an IPO, contact them to ask when you can get the shares. Do not wait until the opening date since that would already be too late.

In an IPO, the shares of stock are limited to each person. This means you can't "hoard" the shares (but there are probably people who work around this). For instance, in the PureGold IPO, the limit was at 1,000 shares per account only.

Is getting into an IPO advisable?

Investing in an IPO entails a lot of risk since the company is usually still new and not all of the information about the company has been 'absorbed' by the public. Add to that the emotional rush it creates - the excitement from everybody wanting to get it and the fear from missing out on an opportunity. This emotional rush makes a lot of investors blind to the risk of not knowing anything about the company.

Imagine this scenario:

Ellie just heard about the IPO of Abakada Company. Ellie is a cautious and patient investor, so she waits for more information before getting into it. Ellie then receives a text from her friend asking, "Will you be buying Abakada IPO?"

Ellie says that she's still thinking about. The friend taunts her, "Don't wait anymore; you should get into it! It's a really good company."

While browsing on Facebook, Ellie sees a post: "Just got in Abakada IPO, woohoo!" She looks at who the post is from, but doesn't recognize the person. It must be one of the random people she added just to get the notifications down to zero.

Later that evening, Ellie went to her Tita's birthday party. While having dinner, she overheard one of the tables talking about investing. It was the "Chinese-Tito's" table.

Since the table was already full, she just tried to listen to their conversation. After a few minutes of listening, she learns that several of them already signed up for the IPO.

The next morning, Ellie calls up her broker and also asks to get her shares for the coming IPO.

Did Ellie learn anything about the company? Not a thing.

What she did find out was that a lot of other people were also getting into it. And that shouldn't be enough reason to justify investing in any company.

I'm very familiar with this scenario since it has happened to me. I got the texts. I saw the posts on Facebook. Instead of a birthday party, it was a Despedida. Instead of the Chinese-tito table, it was my sister's high school friends table. And the moment I signed up for the stocks, I also encouraged my other friends to get into it. Fortunately, I didn't end up losing money.

One of the most lethal get-rich-quick toxins that poisoned the mind of the investing public in the 1990s was the idea you could build wealth by buying IPOs. Investing in an IPO sounds like a great idea – after all, if you had bought 100 shares of Microsoft when it went public in 1986, your $2,100 investment would have grown to $720,000 by early 2003.

Unfortunately, for every IPO like Microsoft that turns out to be a big winner, there are a thousand losers. Psychologists Kahneman and Tversky have shown when humans estimate the likelihood of an event, we make that judgment based not on how often the event has occurred, but on how vivid the past examples are.

We all want to buy "the next Microsoft" – precisely because we know we missed buying the first Microsoft. But we conveniently overlook the fact that most other IPOs were terrible investments.

-from the commentary by Jason Zweig of "The Intelligent Investor" by Benjamin Graham

BASIC STOCK MARKET TERMS

In this section, I'll quickly provide the meaning of basic stock market terms. You'll encounter them as soon as you create your account with an online broker. There will be a bit of technical and boring stuff here, but don't worry about not understanding it at the moment. This is because in part 3 of this e-book, I've provided you with links to step-by-step video and text tutorials on how to go about these items. So, for now, it's enough that you just read through this once to get acquainted with the terms. You'll understand these concepts more when you get started.

Stock Symbol or Stock Code
In the stock market, each company is assigned a nickname (or a code). This is called the stock symbol. You don't need to memorize all of them, since you'll be provided with a 'cheat sheet' when you're making a transaction.

Market Price
The market price is simply the price per share of a particular stock. When the stock market is open, the price can change every second. It all depends on how much the buyers want to buy, and how much the sellers want to sell.

Bid and Ask Price / Size
You will see the bid and ask price when you want to place an order. You will probably see something that looks like

a table. To understand this table of bidding and asking prices, you need to remember that for a transaction to happen, buyers and sellers must "agree" on the price. Naturally, buyers would want to buy at the lowest price possible, while sellers would want to sell at the highest price possible.

This bid/ask table just shows the buyers and sellers meeting point. This is why this table shows the highest buying prices and the lowest selling prices.

Tick Size
The fluctuation or tick size is the smallest increment in the price of a stock. These tick sizes vary depending on the price range that stock belongs to.

If there were no tick sizes, buyers and sellers have an infinite range of prices to bid and sell. This would make it more difficult to facilitate the trades.

Lot Size
Board Lots are also standard increments set by the PSE, but this time the minimum allowable increment affects the number of shares to be bought or sold.

Board Lot
The board lot is simply a table showing the summary of the tick sizes and the lot sizes of the respective price ranges of the stocks.

Limit Orders vs. Market Orders

When you buy or sell using a market order, you pay or receive the current going rate for a stock. Limit orders allow you to set a limit. For example, you can set a highest price you're willing to pay per share and only deal with those willing to sell at that price. This gives you a bit more control - and ensures you get the best deals available.

Whoa! That was a LOT of Technical Information!

Yes, sorry for that! I hope your nose didn't bleed. But don't worry, because you don't have to understand it all at this time. You'll understand it better when you have an account and are going through the actual buying and selling of stocks.

So the technical information you saw up there - we'll go through it in depth with the other step-by-step guides you'll be able to access in Part 3 of this guide. I've made those step-by-step guides in such a way that even a grade school student will be able to follow it – it is a 110% spoon feeding guide. So with that, read on!

ON MORE LEARNING

In this section, you will find my recommended references for further study. I have arranged it in increasing order of complexity (the further down the list, the harder it is to read). So my suggestion is to start doing them from the top of the list per category.

Included in these references are books, e-books, websites, and seminars you can look at to further your learning in those topics. Most of the books listed here at available at National, Power Books or Fully Booked. For the other references, links are provided for more information.

Now, take note that you already know enough to start investing in the stock market. Reading these references below would be good, but it isn't necessary for you to get started. You can do it at the same time you begin investing.

ABUNDANCE MINDSET

"How to Be Truly Rich" Seminar by Bo Sanchez – Ninety percent of money problems are problems of the mind. In this seminar, Bo Sanchez teaches you how to enlarge your "psychological wallet," and prepare your mind to receive abundant blessings. If you join the Truly Rich Club, you already get the recording. (More Information Here)

"Truly Rich Club" Membership by Bo Sanchez – In the Truly Rich Club, you get an overflow of blessings with e-books, audio tapes, seminar recordings, and wealth articles that will guide you in your journey to becoming Truly Rich. In this club, you'll be taught how to be truly rich in all areas of your life: finances, relationships, career, spirituality, and health. (More Information Here)

***The Millionaire Next Door* by Stanley Ph.D. and Danko PhD** – In this book, you'll learn about the wealth habits of the millionaires in America. After reading this, you'll be a lot more conscious of the things that make you richer and the things that make you poorer.

ON INVESTING

***Rich Dad, Poor Dad* by Robert Kiyosaki** – This is the best book that can explain, in very simple terms, how to become rich. It teaches about the difference of real assets and real liabilities. Knowledge of this basic principle will change how you decide what to invest in.

***Who Took My Money* by Robert Kiyosaki** – This book teaches about becoming a more patient investor. Its basic principle is that those who are patient in learning get the highest returns while those who are impatient (want to get the easiest form of investments) get the worst kinds of returns.

***The Intelligent Investor* by Benjamin Graham** – This is a classic when it comes to the world of investing. It teaches "value investing"- a set of principles which guides investors how to become more discerning.

STOCK MARKET: LONG TERM INVESTMENT

***The Turtle Always Wins* by Bo Sanchez** – This is a sequel to "My Maid Invests in the Stock Market." It explains the four kinds of investors in the stock market.

It also shows how and why investing for the long term beats the short term traders.

***Buffetology* by Mary Buffet** – Warren Buffet is the world's greatest investor. In this book, you'll learn about his techniques, which have allowed him to get the greatest returns over long periods.

Warren Buffet and the Interpretation of Financial Statements – This book provides simple explanations of how to understand financial statements. It's a must-read for those who want to take fundamental analysis seriously.

MARKET TIMING, TRADING / TECHNICAL ANALYSIS

COL Technical Analysis Seminars – This is a two-part seminar held once a month by CitisecOnline. Registration is free for current CitisecOnline members. (More Information and Registration Here)

www.Swing–Trade-Stocks.com – This website contains a very structured tutorial on how to time the market. Articles are appropriately separated into beginner, intermediate, and advanced topics.

Other Seminars – I haven't attended all of the seminars available regarding technical analysis. But as a quick guideline here, only attend a technical analysis seminar if that is the ONLY topic for the WHOLE day. Do not attend seminars wherein you'll be taught the basics plus technical analysis, or technical plus fundamental analysis. Technical analysis is a course which is good for a minimum of 8 hours - and that's with a good teacher. That's why the seminar you want to attend should purely be focused on technical analysis alone, for the whole day.

Beating the Market

To start, let me introduce you to Warren Buffett. Mr. Buffett has been the single most successful investor since the late 1950's. Let's set the stage. The year is 1984. Recently, there had arisen a growing consensus that the stock market was fully efficient, called "Efficient Market Theory." Academics and investors were declaring it impossible for someone to consistently pick stocks that would beat the overall market average because everything was priced in already. Columbia Business School hosted an epic debate as a contest between Michael Jensen, a professor from the University of Rochester and one of the leading voices of the Efficient Market Theory, versus Warren Buffett, famed stock-picker. Jensen went first. He argued that if you flipped a coin 50 times, there would be someone that happened to get heads 50 times in a row, but that didn't mean that that person had skill. He called picking stocks a "coin flip."

Ten Buffett spoke. He said "let's imagine that we had a coin-flipping contest. And that, of course, we could have some lucky winners and losers. But then, let's assume that all the winners had something in common.

What if all the winners of the coin-flipping contest came from Omaha, or had an unusual technique? Wouldn't you be curious to find out what made this high concentration of winners? Buffett then went through the investment performance of nine successful investors that just so happened to all practice the same methodology and all had the same teachers, Benjamin Graham and David Dodd. He called them "The Super-Investors of Graham-and-Doddsville." Buffett was unequivocally declared the winner after his masterful speech. No one could doubt the numbers or the logic. The clear conclusion is that you can be successful in picking stocks; and it requires following the investment principles of Graham, Dodd, and Buffett.

Buffett references Benjamin Graham and David L. Dodd. Together, Graham and Dodd wrote *Security Analysis* in 1934. This book, still in print after several editions, has influenced many great investors since the very first YOUNG INVESTORS SOCIETY. Additionally, Benjamin Graham wrote *The Intelligent Investor* in 1949. Mr. Buffett first read this book in 1950 and considers it, "by far the best book on investing ever written." Benjamin Graham is considered the father of value investing, and so we start here. As you read the article make a note of the key concepts that are referenced. Some are repeated several times.

Questions to Consider:
1. What are the common traits of successful investors?
2. If there is a clear recipe for investment success, why do you think so few people follow it?

The Seven Golden Rules

Like any venture, a set of rules can offer guidance in your investments that can lead to greater success. This is one set of rules developed by investing geniuses.

When you are successful in investing in the stock market, you make money. Sometimes a great deal of money. One of the biggest names in the investment world, and one we have studied above, is Warren Buffett. He started by investing $10,000 - and he turned that into a net worth of $60 BILLION!! And he's not the only one. There are many others who have made their fortune in the stock market. You may not have $10,000 in cash to spare. But you can certainly use what you do have to enrich your own net worth.

Rule 1: Think Long-Term

You are unlikely to make millions overnight, or even in the first year or two of investment. You have to look beyond a company's short-term downfalls and into the potential for future growth. For example, American Express stocks took a major hit in 1964. This is when Warren Buffett stepped in and scooped it up. A decade into the future, he didn't regret it.

Rule 2: Good Companies Make Good Investments

Investing in the stock market isn't about having a crystal ball or trying to get ahold of market information a moment before the next person. You can't predict which stocks will grow and when. But, you can identify good companies with solid business plans and invest your money in stocks worthy of it.

- Good Companies:
    - have a unique advantage that isn't easily replicated by competitors.
    - Generate high returns on capital.
    - Don't borrow much money, because their business finances itself.

Rule 3: Buy with a Safety Margin

One of the most-read books by professional investors is Benjamin Graham's *The Intelligent Investor*. This is where the concept of the "Margin of Safety" was introduced. The idea here is that if you buy a business at a low enough price that if you're wrong, your loss would not be significant.

Rule 4: Do Your Own Homework and Know What You Own

You can't take the advice of anyone who comes along when it comes to your investments. You have to know your portfolio and understand the companies you are a part owner in.

Rule 5: Don't Follow the Herd: Stay Calm and Rational

Many investors make the same mistakes - buying when others are buying, and selling when others are selling. This is a strategy that will get you the results of the many. And you're looking to experience the results of the few. Keeping calm is the best way to avoid this downfall.

Rule 6: Don't Put All Your Eggs in One Basket - But Don't have Too Many Baskets, Either

Remember the power of diversification. Having a well-rounded portfolio reduces your risk of taking an overall loss on your investment. But keep in mind the wisdom of studying just a few companies, gaining intimate knowledge of them.

Diversification protects your portfolio from market setbacks. For example, if your entire investment is held up in one corporation that sells beef and the company is plagued by an outbreak of E. coli, you could see a rapid downturn, even possibly a 100% loss! Diversifying helps you balance out the risks of multiple stocks so that one company's loss doesn't in turn lose your entire retirement savings.

One way to diversify investments is to make use of a mutual fund, which holds a basket of investments in a variety of corporations. Using the knowledge base of experts in diversification can earn you a feeling of greater security, though you sacrifice the benefits of being your own broker that we mentioned earlier.

Research shows that 90% of the benefits of diversification can be obtained with a portfolio of just over 20 stocks. Once you diversify further, you begin to have less knowledge and understanding of the companies you're working with.

Diversify, but remember you want to invest only in those companies you believe in, rather than building a varied portfolio of companies you're not so sure about.

Rule 7: Never Stop Learning

This is probably the most important rule - in stock market investing as well as in life. You can never learn too much about topics that interest you. Even the greatest investors take the opportunity to learn from one another. Warren Buffett credits much of his success to other investors such as Charlie Munger and Benjamin Graham.

BONUS: Find Meaningful Ways to Give Back

Often we hear more about the most wealthy among us because of their efforts at giving back to the community than we hear about their financial successes. Bill and Melinda Gates have dedicated much of their fortune to battling poverty and improving the quality of education across the nation and throughout the world. Warren Buffett has committed his billions to improving life for others around him, rather than simply padding his own bank account. You don't have to make billions to give back. You can commit a percentage of your earnings to a charity of your choice. Or simply use some of the time your healthier financial situation has lent you to donate your time to those in need.

Thank you and I hope you enjoy this audiobook, the only thing is I ask is if you could please leave a review after listening.

SECTION 3 –STOCK MARKET - VALUES!

Imagine in front of you is a box containing a dozen doughnuts. How much would you pay for one donut? If all the donuts in the box are the same, is one worth more than the other? What if the world had a shortage of sugar and this was the last box of donuts in the world, with none being able to be made for the next year, does the scarcity increase the value of the good? How about if you just ate a box of donuts and can't eat anymore, does the value you would pay for a donut decrease?

The box of 12 doughnuts represents a company. When you break the company down, everyone has an opportunity to own some of the donuts, or part of the company. But people may pay wildly different prices for the same donut. If you want to maximize the value of a box of donuts, what might be the best approach? One method is to convince people that these are the tastiest donuts in the world and they will only be around for a limited time. In a nutshell, this is how the market works. The stock market is made up of people who get excited about something or sick of something depending on their mood. What is obvious is that occasionally the market goes nuts!

What Is The Value Of A Business?

We'll only invest in a company when the price we pay today is significantly less than the value we will get tomorrow.

Example: A teacher picks a student at random. The teacher holds up a $10 bill and asks the student, "What is the value of this bill?" Ten dollars. The teacher holds up ten $1 bills. She asks the same question, "What is the value of these dollar bills?" Ten dollars. The teacher offers to sell the student the $10 bill for the ten 1 dollar bills. This is a wash, so maybe he'll take it, maybe he won't.

Then the Teacher offers to sell the $10 for only five 1 dollar bills. Of course, he should take it. Ask the question to the rest of the class at large, "How many of you would buy this?" Do the reverse. Ask to sell the $10 bill for twenty $1 bills? How many would take this? None of them.

The best investors can snatch up $10 bills when the market is only asking $5 for them. But how is this possible? It is possible because a. the value is tricky to calculate, and b. the market is irrational.

Remember the Market goes nuts. Is this a good thing or a bad thing for you? It's a very good thing. If all investors based their investment decisions on rational and conservative estimates of intrinsic value, it would be very difficult to make money in the stock market. Fortunately, the participants in the stock market are humans subject to the corroding influence of emotions.

Many investors will give into the hype around stocks, or people will hop on a trend because they have optimistic views that they can beat the system. As young investment geniuses, we will always check emotions at the door and buy stocks based on what they are worth.

Understanding the Terminology
A company's worth – which is its total value – is called its market capitalization and it is represented by the company's stock price. Market cap (as it is commonly referred to) is equal to the stock price multiplied by the number of shares outstanding.

For example, a stock with a $5 stock price and 10 million shares outstanding/trading is worth $50 million ($5 x 10 million). If we take this one step further, we can see that a company that has a $10 stock price and one million shares outstanding (market cap = $10 million) is worth less than a company with a $5 stock price and 10 million shares outstanding (market cap = $50 million).

Thus, the stock price is a relative and proportional value of a company's worth and only represents percentage changes in market cap at any given point in time. Any percentage changes in a stock price will result in an equal percentage change in a company's value. This is the reason investors are so concerned with stock prices and any changes that may occur since even a $0.10 drop in a $5 stock can result in a $100,000 loss for shareholders with one million shares.

Questions To Consider:
1. What is the Market Cap of a Company with a stock price of $20/share and 10 million shares outstanding?
2. What is the current Market Cap of Apple? How many shares do they have outstanding and what is the stock price?

The next logical question is: Who sets stock prices and how are they calculated? In simple terms, the stock price of a company is calculated when a company goes on sale to the public; an event called an initial public offering.

This is when a company will pay an investment bank a lot of money to use very complex formulas and valuation techniques to derive a company's value by determining how many shares will be offered to the public and at what price. For example, a company whose value is estimated at $100 million may want to issue 10 million shares at $10 per share, or they may want to issue 20 million at $5 a share.

As we saw in the example with Apple, a company's value is dependent on how much the company can grow its earnings in the future. When a company sells more items or enters a new market or improves margins, it can grow profits.

The "Go-To" Way to Value a Business: P/E Ratio
One way to determine the value of a business is with the Price-to-Earnings Ratio or P/E Ratio.

The price-earnings ratio can be calculated as:
Market Value per Share (Stock Price) / Earnings per Share

For example, suppose that a company is currently trading at $43 a share and its earnings over the last 12 months were $1.95 per share. The P/E ratio for the stock could then be calculated as $43/$1.95, or about 22x.

In essence, the price-earnings ratio indicates how many years an investor has to wait at the current earnings to get all their money back. If the P/E ratio is 22x, you are saying at this level of earnings; it will take you 22 years for the company to earn how much you bought the stock for $43. In general, a high P/E suggests that investors are expecting higher earnings growth in the future compared to companies with a lower P/E. A low P/E can indicate either a company may currently be undervalued or the company's profits are expected to decline.

Think of a P/E as the price you pay for a stock.

In general, there are a couple of Price / Earnings (P/E) rules of thumb:

The average P/E over the past decade is 15. An average company, should be worth about 15.

Really great companies (very high returns with consistent earnings growth) tend to trade about 20-25x P/E.

Bad companies, ones whose earnings are unpredictable and make low returns, usually trade at below 10x P/E.

A company should trade at about the P/E as its earnings are expected to grow in the future. Companies growing profits 30% per year may be justified to trade at 30x P/E. Companies growing 15% per year may trade at 15x P/E. Companies not growing may trade at 5-10x P/E.

As you can see, valuing stocks is like going to a grocery store. You get what you pay for. If you want to buy the best product, you're likely going to have to pay for it.

There are two reasons to buy companies with a low P/E ratio:
- The company may be undervalued.
- The company most likely has high earnings.

Key Takeaways
1. Stocks fluctuate wildly on a yearly basis. The true value of the business does not actually change much.
2. If someone offers you a dollar for fifty cents, take it!
3. The two most important things that determine the value of a company are: a. how much profits are going to grow to, and b. how long that profit level is sustainable.
4. The P/E ratio is a good starting point to determine the value of a company.

What Makes A Good Business?

Think finding a good long-term business is easy? Just take a quick look at history, and you'll see that only a handful of companies survive over time. For example, create a list of businesses that have failed or gone bankrupt in the past 20 years. (Examples: Chrysler, Enron, Delta Airlines, Countrywide Mortgages, and Lehman Brothers)   Why do you think that some companies succeed while others fail? How can we identify the winners from the losers for investment purposes?

How do I Know if a Company is a Good Business?

Economic Moats

When we think of moats, we may envision the body of water surrounding a castle or fortress. The economic moat is essentially the same. It is a type of protection a company holds from external forces. There are many types, and each are excellent indicators that a company is a great place to invest your money. Below are the different types of moats:

- **Intangible Assets:** Brands, patents, and regulatory licenses may allow a company to sell products or services that can't be replicated by competitors.
- **High Switching Costs:** Products and services offered to consumers on a contract can make it difficult for those consumers to switch to another company, providing some power in pricing and additional economic security.
- **Network Effect:** Some companies benefit from network economics, one of the most powerful

moats. The network effect means that the more consumers are in the network, the better the value they find in the product or service. It is mutually beneficial to both the company and the consumer, which also creates a strong sense of loyalty.

- **Low-Cost Advantage:** Some companies experience certain advantages that cause them to be able to offer their goods and services at a cost much lower than competing companies, which offers a lasting economic moat.

Learning Check:
1. What is a company that comes to mind when you think of those with a wide and powerful moat? What company is likely to stand strong 10 years from now.
2. What is a company with a narrow moat? What company is currently doing well, but you don't see standing the test of time.
3. Now, what about a company in which you can't identify any moat at all? What company is just a bad business both now and in the future.

Quick Matching Game:
The following companies have stood the test of time, which probably indicates they have some sort of economic moat. Can you identify what their economic moat is? (intangible assets, high switching costs, network effect, low cost advantage)
- Coca Cola
- Bank of America
- Google

- Wal-Mart
- Exxon Mobil

Hint: *There can be more than one per company!*

Conclusion

All businesses are not created equal: some are bad, most are average, but some are really, really good. Selling candy is better than selling rats, and even better is selling Coca-Cola or iPhones. The goal of the long term investor is to identify really good companies that can earn high returns on capital for decades into the future. The only way to defend these high returns though is with a deep economic moat.

The surest way to make money in the stock market is to invest in good companies that make exceptional returns and can defend these returns for decades into the future. In this lesson, you have learned how to identify these companies. If you master this skill, you will gain one of the most valuable investing tools a great investor will ever learn.

Key Takeaways:
- ❖ Most businesses will fail.
- ❖ There are some exceptional businesses out there that have an "economic moat".
- ❖ Great companies have the economic moats of Intangible Assets / Brands, High Switching Costs, Network Effects or a Low Cost Advantage.

❖ Don't open a rat store.

Warren Buffett
"Time is the friend of the wonderful company, the enemy of the mediocre."

SECTION FOUR: LEAP!

Now that you already know everything you need to begin investing in the stock market, I'll be showing you the specific steps you should take to get started. In this section, please note that my focus is the action step itself, so I will no longer elaborate on ideas which have been discussed in part 1 and part 2 of this guide.

I will only give specific instructions which will move you further along your journey in investing.

My goal here is to get you started with your investments in the fastest and most effective way possible.

So bear in mind that rather than present you with Options A, B and C, I will just instruct you to do X, Y and then Z.

Day 1: Commit to a Personal Investing Goal

The first thing that you will need to get started is your commitment. While that's such a cliché statement, it needs to be said – and repeated. Nothing will happen without your commitment.

Right now, it doesn't matter if you're rich or poor, a college graduate or a drop-out, an employee or an entrepreneur. It doesn't matter where you're coming from – all that matters is where you're going. So at this moment, the only thing that matters is if you're willing to improve your financial life and start investing in the stock market.

With that said, I'd like you to commit to a goal that you will be moving toward financial freedom. It could be about investing for yourself, or for the people you love. The important thing here is that you decide and commit to it.

Creating Your Personal Investing Goal!
First, write down your **WHY**! The most important thing is to know why you're investing. Are you investing so that you can enjoy a carefree retirement? Are you hoping to retire early? Do you want to send your children to college debt-free? Purchase a home in cash? Leave behind a legacy for your family? This is what you will need to keep in mind throughout your investing adventure.

Write down your personal investing goal and put it where you'll see it frequently. This way, every time you see it, you'll be reminded of the promise you have made to yourself. Commit to yourself. Know that you are worth the effort. You are worth the risk. And your outcomes are within your control.

Here is a sample of a goal you might write. You'll notice it contains the investment goal, which is cut and dry (10% or more of salary). If you simply commit to investing in general without an amount in mind, setting aside the funds for investment will not maintain the level of priority it requires. You'll also notice that written within the goal is the WHY. Without remembering why we are making a choice, again, the level of priority will downshift. Your plans for investment in the stock market will be much like your last New Year's Resolution - likely forgotten within the first month.

I am consistently investing 10% or more of my salary so that I can comfortably retire and spend more time with the people I love and care about.

Day 2: Create an Account with CitisecOnline or your broker of choice.

Now, it's time to move forward and create an account with CitisecOnline (or the broker you choose). We have listed online brokers in another section of this book. Each have their advantages and disadvantages. Make sure to do your homework. You can find comparison charts online listing the features, fees, and what traders love or hate about working with them.

It may take 2-3 days for COLFinancial (or the online broker of your choice) to process your forms from the time they receive them. So it's really good if you start as soon as possible. One of my friends told me that she didn't act on this very quickly when she was starting. She was already excited to get started, but for some reason, she only filled out the forms and never sent them to COLFinancial. Then, without her knowing, several months passed by with her forms accumulating dust in the drawer. Now, I hope you don't let this happen to you. So act now, act now, and act now.

Check in daily and have the funds available and ready to invest. Be excited and count down the days until your account is active and you are ready to trade! Have your plan in place. Know what you're planning to buy and what you're willing to pay. Practice tracking the stocks while you wait and build the anticipation. This is an exciting new journey you're about to begin!

Day 3: Try Out or Sign-up To the Truly Rich Club (Or Another Service)

In my opinion, Truly Rich Club is the best guide out there for beginners and even veterans. You have worked hard for your money, and I think your money deserves the best "babysitter" (Edward Lee) out there. Ultimately, what this can mean for you is not only profitability, but peace of mind. To know that you're being guided by the best means you can sleep soundly while your money works hard for you.

Now, I think of the Truly Rich Club as being able to hire the best stock market expert here in the Philippines (Edward Lee) so that he can tell me exactly what to buy and sell.

There are many similar services available online. Again, you'll want to do your homework to determine which is the best fit for you and your needs. There are U.S. based agencies as well. Different investment experts have different approaches. Take a peak at a few different ones and see who aligns best with your goals and priorities.

However, if paying for expert guidance is not your thing, another other option is to look at the COL EIP recommendation list. As of Nov 2012, they are recommending 16 different companies that you can invest in for the long term. Now, please take note here that with this COL EIP list, you will be on your own. So it's important that you have the discipline and confidence to keep on investing in your selected companies.

If you can't decide at the moment, then just go for the Truly Rich Club and try it out. There's a 30-day money back guarantee anyway. So you can just "see what it's like" first.

Day 4: Buy your First Stock
From your list from the TRC or EIP, pick out a company that you like and buy it. Two to three companies from different industries would be a good enough diversification at this point. Start out small and consistently make additional purchases to build your portfolio as you get the hang of it. You'll learn as you go. You'll also build confidence along the way that will help guide your activities.

Day 5: Monitor Your Investment
Congratulations!

You are invested in the stock market.

Feel free to watch your investments go green (up), and go red (down). The important thing to remind yourself here is that you are a long-term investor and that these small price movements don't matter.

Right now, you should be proud that business tycoons are working hard to make your money grow. (Recall that if you buy a stock, you are buying into a business, and you are leveraging on the people running that business.) While those working for the company are hard at work, your money is doing your work for you.

Day 6: Stick to Your Investing Strategy
Next month or next quarter, make sure to invest your savings into the stock market. Remember that your original investment grows if you don't keep on planting. It doesn't matter how small you put in every month; the important thing is that you are accumulating wealth.

Now, as you begin to invest in the stock market, you will notice that a lot of people will be boasting about their investing strategies. You will hear about people making 50+% over the past month, and it's natural to get a little envious of this.

But it is at this point that you need to stick to your strategy because of the following reasons:
1. You do not know how much money these people have lost in the past. Most probably they are only sharing their wins.
2. You do not know how long these people study the stock market, and how exactly they study it. They may be spending several hours a day so they can execute their trades.

3. You do not know what kind of rules they follow with their trades.
4. You do not know when they bought that stock or when they sold it.

If you want to venture into a new strategy, you need to preserve your current strategy, and just set aside a portion for this adventure. For example, if you're investing $2000 monthly, you can divide that amount into two portions: The first portion is for your slow but sure way of investing, and the other portion is for the new strategy. In this manner, you secure your core long-term investment, while you get to explore other strategies.

Day 7: Share the Knowledge
This isn't surprising, considering we were never taught how to invest. Our teachers didn't teach us, nor did our parents. After all, how could they teach us if no one taught them, either?

I am saying this to you so that you can appreciate the person who introduced you to the stock market and made you download this book. Thank that person, because the knowledge that you gained here is so very rare.

I sincerely hope that since you're almost done reading this book, you will be investing in the Stock Market within the week (or at most within the month). And when you finally get to start investing in the stock market, hopefully you can share the knowledge here.

This way, sometime in the future, the majority of working-class individuals will have the much-deserved convenience of making their money work hard for them. Let's end the poverty. Let's spread financial literacy. It is one thing to learn how to invest and grow your wealth. As with anything, we know we have truly learned, on the highest level, when we are able to teach others.

The BONUS step we discussed earlier was the importance of giving back once you've made your fortune. One sure way to give back is to help others create wealth through investing in the stock market.

Investing in Your Future

As you continue your journey into investing in the stock market, keep in mind the discussion we had in the first section of this book about your financial future. Upon retirement, will you have 30+ years of expenses available to you? Or will you be living a life filled with stress and uncertainty? Will you be enjoying a much-earned life of leisure, traveling and spending quality time with family and friends? Or will you be working full time long into your golden years, until you've reached a point of exhaustion that doesn't allow for fulfilling the lifelong dreams you had always assumed you would have time for later on?

For the vast majority of working-class individuals, Social Security benefits and the retirement plan offered by our employers are simply not enough to sustain comfortable lifestyles. Yet if we start now, putting our money to work for us, we could be in a much better financial situation, potentially even able to leave behind a legacy for our beloved family members.

Remember – if you are currently in debt, eliminating your debt is your first priority. Money owed creates more money owed and paying interest and fees on your debt will counteract any good you're doing yourself in investments. Handle the debt first – and invest only the money you won't need in the near future.

Initial investments can be small. You may consider adding to your portfolio in small, frequent amounts. You may not miss just $50 per month that you commit to investing. But over time, even small sums add up, especially when given time to grow. Watching your money grow will give you the confidence and the added motivation to begin investing more. You may find ways to cut back on spending so that you have more available to invest. And all investments made work for you toward the goals you've set for yourself and your future.

Advice from Investment Experts
Let's hear from some of the many men and women who have made millions (even billions) investing in the stock market.

"Investors should purchase stocks like they purchase groceries, not like they purchase perfume"
- *Ben Graham*

One can find two distinct interpretations here.

- You MUST prioritize your investment goals as you would those chores most important to you.
- Keep in mind the companies that are most secure are those offering the essentials - grocery markets are relatively recession-proof.

"We try to avoid buying a little of this or that when we are only lukewarm about the business or its price. When we are convinced as to attractiveness, we believe in buying worthwhile amounts."
-   *Ben Graham*

Diversification is powerful - but remember not to overdo it.

"You get recessions, you have stock market declines. If you don't understand that's going to happen, then you're not ready, you won't do well in the markets."
-   *Peter Lynch*

Keep in mind the fluidity of the market and the inherent changes. Don't stress too much about short-term declines. Remember the stock market is a long-term investment.

"The stock market is a device for transferring money from the impatient to the patient."
-   *Warren Buffett*

Patience, patience, patience. You won't make your fortune overnight - you have to learn to take small losses in stride and focus on the long-term.

"An important key to investing is to remember that stocks are not lottery tickets."
> -   *Peter Lynch*

The stock market won't make you rich overnight. But then, you have a much higher probability of earning money in the stock market than in the lottery.

"Take charge of your financial future. I believe investing small amounts each month in the stock market will give you financial freedom in the later years of your life."
> -   *Bo Sanchez*

As we have before, look ahead to the years after you leave your 9-5 job and begin to live the life you deserve! Consistent investments over time will feel like less of a sacrifice and maintaining the habit will compound your earnings.

"Only buy something that you'd be perfectly happy to hold if the market shut down for ten years."
> -   *Warren Buffett*

We simply can't overemphasize the important of thinking long-term in your investments. Don't buy stocks in the next hot trend if you don't see the company as having true staying power.

"Learn every day, but especially from the experiences of others. It's cheaper!"
- *John Bogle*

Take advantage of the resources available to you to avoid the mistakes others have made and capitalize on strategies that have been proven effective by the best in the field!

"Price is what you pay. Value is what you get."
- *Warren Buffett*

Don't be tempted to load up on only the least expensive stocks. Remember to pay attention to the value of the company and think about it's staying power. As the saying goes, you get what you pay for.

"In many ways, the stock market is like the weather in that if you don't like the current conditions, all you have to do is wait a while."
- *Low Simpson*

One thing you can absolutely count on is that there will be constant change. Again, patience is your best virtue in the stock market. Do your best to wait out the storm and be rewarded at the end of the rainbow.

"In the business world, the rear-view mirror is always cleaner than the windshield."
- *Warren Buffett*

Isn't this just true of life in general? Don't beat yourself up, thinking you should have predicted your losses. Hindsight, as they say, is 20/20. And the stock market, like life, is inherently unpredictable.

"You have to know what you own, and why you own it."
- *Peter Lynch*

Remember to do your own homework. Always know what you're invested in. And keep in mind your *why*.

"Individuals who cannot master their emotions are ill-suited to profit from the investment process."
- *Benjamin Graham*

If you are an overly-anxious person, investment in the stock market may prove emotionally difficult for you. There are many unknowns and a great deal of patience is required to meet you investment goals.

"The game of life is the game over everlasting learning. At least it is if you want to win."
- *Charlie Munger*

You can never stop learning! Always, always, always seek out new knowledge that will lead to better future investments.

"Everyone has the power to follow the stock market. If you made it through fifth grade math, you can do it."
- *Peter Lynch*

As we discussed before, there is a plethora of terminology and it can seem very complicated, but once you get to know it, understanding the stock market is quite simple.

"It's far better to buy a wonderful company at a fair price than a fair company at a wonderful price."

- *Warren Buffett*

True in life as in stock market investment, it's important to consider quality over quantity. Keep in mind that cost and value are separate when you're making decision about which companies to purchase.

"Without a saving faith in the future, no one would ever invest at all. To be an investor, you must be a believer in a better tomorrow."

- *Benjamin Graham*

Hope for a better future is what investment is all about!

Conclusion

Now that you've finished reading this book, I just want to let you know that you already know so much. What took me six whole months to understand, you just read in the past hour or so. And believe me when I tell you this: You are READY. You already have what it takes to be an investor. All you have to do now is take a step forward by following the steps and guides above.

Having read this book, you should have more confidence in your ability to begin making transactions in the stock market. You should know where to find quality advice and some basic terminology that will help you successfully navigate whichever online brokerage firm you choose to use. Your journey in stock market investing is new. But remember to trust yourself and your instincts. Do your homework and get to know and understand the companies you're part-owner in. Make a plan for what to do with dividends. Will you cash them out and treat yourself to something special, or reinvest them so that you can capitalize on those gains? You should now know what are reasons you find good enough to invest in a company, as well as what reasons you may find to sell stock in one. You have your goals set and all that's left to do is commit. This is an exciting time! Don't forget to enjoy the journey to financial freedom! And don't be afraid to dream of the amazing future you can have!

With that, I'd like to ask a little something from you. I would like for you to read the words below aloud. It may sound corny - but do it anyway. These words summarize who you have become in the process of reading this book (and well, it's also an awesome way of ending the book too!) So are you ready? Let's say this all together now.

"I am no longer a slave to money. I am free.
I am no longer a spender, and I am better than a saver.
I am an investor. And I make my money work hard for me!"

P.S. I enjoyed writing this book, and I hope you enjoyed reading it too. Please feel free to share

ENDING CREDITS (PLEASE MAKE INTO ITS OWN FILE)

If you enjoyed this audiobook, you might like our other book "Real Estate Investing For Beginners: Make Money Investing In Real Estate And Generate Passive Income, Wealth & Financial Freedom (With Flipping, Commercial, Rental Property & Realtor Business Ideas)"

We will give you a preview of the first 2 chapters to see if it is something that you will also like, so here it is:

Chapter One

Real Estate: The Pathway to Sustainable Wealth

There has been a real estate boom that has caused a lot of people to refocus their attention on the market, and now more people are aware of the authenticity of wealth via real estate proceeds. But, is this boom enough to create sustainable wealth?

When we speak of wealth that is sustainable, we refer to long-lasting and impactful wealth that transcends generations. What else will make for sustainable wealth if not homes and land properties?

Come on, look around you; everywhere you turn, there is a house. We live, survive, and connect based on what we have as properties. The thought of being able to make money off real estate ought to make you extremely excited, because it has great rewards.

More than ever today, more people are attempting to become real estate moguls, and all of them strive to use techniques that will work for them. This has led to a surge in the number of books on real estate. However, it is advisable that you join the wagon with wisdom.

Real estate markets are known for being unstable. As such, every investor (novice or experienced) must become conversant with the principles of successful investing before going ahead with any investment plans.

Without a doubt, the real estate market is beautiful, because when you do make a profit over outstanding sales, it is always a good one. Unlike other sectors in which you may be unsure about the status of your investment despite challenging times, one thing is sure; properties always sell!

So, if you invest in some properties, it is possible to hold off on selling them until you find the right buyer who offers a great price. Should anything happen to a property or investor (accidents or death), the family of that investor can reap a neat profit from the property or pass it on to future generations.

I want you to know that you are on the right path in your search for true, lasting wealth. But, there is a lot of work to be done and many concepts to learn, first.

I always like to share the story of Zuri, a close friend who utilised the ideas shared in this book to make her first real estate investment move. At the time Zuri implemented what she learned, this book wasn't even in print; I just shared the ideas with her and boom! - she put them to work.

Zuri had to follow through with all the ideas we had discussed. She recognised the importance of matching the ideas with actions (which is so essential). And, five years later, Zuri is the proud owner of 12 properties.

I know you are imagining how much she's going to make already with twelve properties, but the number of features isn't the main attraction with this story. What I love about Zuri's story is the fact that she was able to turn those action plans into a success story. It really wouldn't matter if it were just one property she secured; what matters is the fact that with focus and a determined mind, she achieved and surpassed her goals.

So - why real estate? Why should anyone rely on real estate as a source of passive income? Read on to get answers.

The Benefits of Real Estate for Wealth Creation

1. It is a sure means for passive income.
Passive income is money you gain without having to go to work every day; it is money you don't actively work for. As such, it is the best form of income anyone could aspire to enjoy. You are not considered wealthy until you have a lot of avenues for passive income.

Wealth shouldn't be something you struggle to achieve, nor should it be something that makes you work too hard. You should just put in the work, and it should yield the right results; this is what real estate offers you.

2.   Properties always appreciate.
Regardless of how challenging it will be, properties will still appreciate. This is one advantage of real estate investment that makes it very appealing. Zuri isn't bothered about the state of her properties because she knows that whenever she is ready to sell, she will make a profit.

Several investment platforms have a cloud of uncertainty around them; their volatile nature makes it increasingly difficult for people to enjoy the dividends of their investments. An excellent example of such uncertain investments is stocks and shares. But with real estate, you won't have to deal with such issues - especially now that you have this definitive guide with you.

3.   Diversification leads to stability.
Real estate diversifies your investment portfolio. This is good, but what is even more interesting is the fact that it can also lead to security in your collection.

When you become an investor, you shouldn't seek assets in just one sector; you can diversify and do more with what you have through various channels.

With real estate, your portfolio is broadened. You experience stability, because when other investments are unstable, your properties bring in a balance that strengthens the portfolio. This feature of real estate investment is crucial to wealth creation.

4. Increased cash flows.

Due to increase in values, your cash flows will also experience the same growth. You have the choice to increase prices on your property and match it up with the current price in the market, and this gives you access to cash whenever you want it.

In a chapter ahead, we will be dealing with the concept of being a landlord. That chapter throws further insight into how real estate aids cash flow. Before we get to that section, you should know that real estate investments will increase your cash flow.

5. Title ownership.

With real estate investment, you also get to enjoy the title ownership of properties. You OWN the properties and decide what you want to do with them. Some people get into severe financial trouble and search for assets to sell off to fix their issues. Yet, because they do not own anything, they are unable to help themselves.

If you invest in real estate, you will have an opportunity to win something that increases in value over time. The most remarkable feeling that wealth gives you is the knowledge of being able to get what you need when you need it; this is a summary of how valuable real estate can be.

6. Transferrable wealth.

Some investments are not transferrable; and this has enormous implications for people who want to invest for their families, spouses, kids, and other third parties.

However, real estate is transferrable. That means you can invest today and transfer the property with its value to another person. It is safe to say that investment in real estate is the gift that keeps on giving; it is a perfect gift idea for someone you love.

More importantly, the fact that it is transferrable also means you can create a legacy of wealth others can build on for a very long time.

7. Tax benefits.

It is possible to get tax deductions on your mortgage interest as you invest in real estate. The tax deductions also apply to cash flows from investment properties, operating expenses, and costs. Insurance and depreciation are not left out in tax deductions.

So, when you start investing, you might want to wrap up all your deals before the year runs out. The end of the year is always a busy time for real estate, as it is an opportunity to utilise all the tax benefits.

With investments in real estate, there are no actual losses; you may have the occasional experiences that every investor has with a stake, but there is one sure thing; you will make a profit.

Over the years, the real estate industry has grown in value as everyone is trying to get their hands on it. You have reached the advantage over everyone else because you are armed with the right tools, knowledge, and information on how this works. So, be prepared to win and get ready to achieve a whole lot with this book.

Since there is an ever-increasing appeal with the real estate market, so many people jump right in and expect instantaneous results. When the results don't pour in as expected, they become frustrated and term the real estate sector "DIFFICULT." Well, I don't think Zuri would have made the kind of progress she did if she had not been patient. Five years is a long time - and Zuri had to wait.

So, in a bid to show you the importance of waiting, we will be heading right over to the next chapter, which will teach you all about the pitfalls of the "get-rich-quick" approach. It is an enlightening chapter that will lead us right into the central conversations of how to invest and succeed with real estate.

Chapter Two

Avoiding the "Get-Rich-Quick" Approach

Lasting wealth takes time to grow; every successful person who shares their story with you will tell you that it took a lot of time for them to arrive at the level of success they now enjoy. The same principle applies to real estate investment.

If you are going to reap the rewards of this approach to investment, then you must get rid of the "get-rich-quick" method. In this chapter, we will consider what the approach is and proffer solutions on how you can be refocused on your investment goals without expecting instant results.

For a person to build wealth quickly, they must do things slowly. There has to be a process of thinking before action is taken. This process helps you weigh all options, thus clearing the pathway for increased success with your investment.

A lot of investors are lured into real estate because they see how many other people excel at it; what they fail to recognise and apply is the fact that these successful people invest an equal amount of time and effort to ensuring that they accomplish their set goals.

For some other successful investors, it was just pure luck.

So if you are considering winning with your real estate investment portfolio, you have to be ready to work on it long term. Those who try to achieve success at once are often disappointed, frustrated, and lose the motivation to continue with their investment.

Simply put - there are no shortcuts to succeeding with real estate. You must imbibe two principles for long-term success; and they are **patience** and **hard work**. Some investors learn a new trick and instantly want to use it to reach the peak. After a few weeks, they realise it won't work and must start all over again.

Some other investors observe a pattern of successful investors and apply it, albeit in a common way. The point is, if you do not put in the same effort, you will not get the same results. The sooner you get the idea of "get-rich-quick" out of your mind, the better off you'll be.

Real estate is like weight loss; everyone talks about it, a lot of people try to make it work, but only a few experience the effects of weight loss. There are millions of people in the real estate and weight loss industry, but only a few get to the peak.

With weight loss, you are told to do straightforward things such as exercise and eat fruits and vegetables, yet the process itself isn't simple. Anyone who has tried to lose weight will tell you it is a serious challenge; it is so severe that some people give up midway into their weight loss programs. In the midst of the struggle, some people come on television to testify about the effect of the process in their lives.

So, sitting in your home and watching those testimonials will cause you to wonder if there is something you are doing wrong. The weight loss experience isn't a fraudulent one; you are just not putting in the required effort and work needed; and until you do, your weight will be a struggle.

Too many people are impatient; it is the reason they don't get the results they seek. If you are serious about losing weight, the same way you are passionate about succeeding in real estate, you will follow through with the process regardless of how long it takes.

There are some steps you can take toward ensuring that your philosophy about real estate doesn't deviate to the "get-rich-quick" pattern. Below, you will find the steps you should consider.

How to Achieve Real Estate Investment Plans

1. Set realistic goals.

First, you must have goals. For anything significant to succeed, you must have a plan - and your goals form the springboard of your projects. So, if you are prepared to succeed, you have to sit still and curate plans that focus on how you want to execute your real estate business.

With your goals in hand, you will have a compass that drives and propels you forward - even in challenging times. Before you launch out to begin your real estate adventure, take the time to set goals.

2. Work hard.

Now, the importance of this cannot be overemphasised. You must work hard to ensure that your goals come to fruition. Your goals give you the motivation you hope for the future, but hard work is what makes a dream come true.

Every day, do something that takes you closer to the realisation of your goals. For every effort you make, you will be rewarded with success. So, work hard and put in your best work toward your goals.

3. Be patient.

As you curate goals and work hard, remember to exercise patience. Do not be in a hurry to get results, because impatience makes people miss out on something good. You should imbibe the culture of tolerance that enables you to hold on to something until it works out for you.

Tell yourself you are not going to give up until the results start to trickle in. An investor who wants to succeed must be patient; this is a rule that is true of all investment sectors.

4. Focus on quality, not quantity.

A lot of times, investors are in a hurry to excel. As such, they start buying properties. Oh! They buy a lot of features in a bid to show how "successful" they are. Going for quantity over quality is always the wrong approach.

Instead of buying many properties that aren't valuable, it is advisable that you stick with quality over quantity. It is better to have one house that is an asset positioned to increase in value within a specified period than have several properties that are undervalued. Always remember this; stick to quality over quantity.

5. Education + action = success.

Next, you need to educate yourself on the principles and steps to take for successful real estate investment. However, education is not enough; it is crucial that you match your education with actionable steps.

Education + action is the combination that leads to success as a real estate investor. So as much as you are committed to learning, be focused on acting as well. Everything you read, starting with this book, should come to life and work for you.

6. Continue learning

You must continue learning so you always have ways through which you can stay motivated and forget about the "get-rich-quick" pattern. If you had not read this book, you probably wouldn't have gotten all of the ideas you have now.

Read more books and continue to inspire yourself with words and plans. Books, mailing lists, podcasts, etc. are all avenues for learning you can utilize.

7. Aspire and emulate.

Don't just look up to others; make up your mind that you are going to be like them. So first, you must develop the aspirations to be like the successful investors you see - and then emulate them by putting in the same kind of work they put into their investments.

The pattern to success doesn't end with aspirations alone; act, fail, learn, fail, and continue until it is perfected.

8. Observe the trends.

Trends help us decipher what is working and what isn't. You must observe the real estate market, the same way you track your shares and stocks.

By not observing trends, you will be listening to speculations from non-investors - or unprofessional ones who want to get instant cash. Follow the pattern by following other original investors like yourself; you will get to know what's happening within seconds.

9. Avoid magic bullets.

Magic bullets refer to quick fixes people look for to succeed; they are not the steps that lead to sustainable wealth, nor are they the approaches that will lead to long-term success.

Magic bullets will make it difficult for you to see the bigger picture. As such, they must be avoided at all costs. Magic bullets make it all seem very easy; but in no time, it will come crashing down on you.

10. Reach out to someone else.

They say the best way to learn on a deeper level is to teach what you know. If you recall Zuri's story, it will interest you to know that I gained a lot from her when she came back and said she had used my principles.

If you want all of these lessons to become a part of your long-term strategy, you need to find someone who is also willing to embark on this journey – and teach that person all you know. While sharing your ideas, you will also learn a thing or two.

Some people want to get involved with real estate one day and start making a lot of money the following day. This book is going to empower you to think differently. You can achieve all you desire; but first, there are things you must put in place to ensure that you are on the right path to success.

Follow the steps you've got above carefully, plan, and execute; you will be amazed at how far you go with your real estate investment. With real estate, some people think it is just about buying and selling houses. There are numerous ways through which you can generate wealth - and we are going to discover them in the next chapter.

Section Five:

Investment Strategies: How To Win On The Stock Market

As a shareholder or stock owner, your major priority should lie on your stocks. On how to make them more valuable or even increase their number. The aim of every investor is to gain profit and not the other way around (lose profit). So the question now remains, how does one really tackle and exploit the obstacles and strengths the Stock Market comes with to our advantage?

The Stock Market and Stock business had been quite popular over the years with lots of people delving into this line of investments. So what do the Stock Market really entails? We'll enlighten you. The Stock Market contains stocks and shareholders (i.e. Real-time investors). Stocks are more like shares or even equity as they can be used in place of each other.

An owner of stock is entitled to a certain part of the company as regards assets or earnings. Now, every stock investor would always have it in mind to learn strategies, ways, and even techniques in improving their investments and always winning in the Stock Market. Be rest assured, there are lots of books, internet materials, factual contents, and so much more which you can find out useful tips as regards this subject matter.

However, what these books, internet materials, and contents won't do is to go into full details and explicitly walk you through these techniques, ways, and strategies. Additionally, the kinds of strategies we execute solely depend on the situation surrounding our investment. The decisions we are going to always take concerning our stock investment ls always depends largely on the factors that influence it.

That way, we would be sure not to fall into any form of miscalculation and risks that would sink our investment. These factors are as follows.

1.   Investor's Pocket: This is a very important factor that influences the decisions of an investor. An investor knows better than to start what he or she can't finish. While embarking on a strategy towards improving and increasing your stock value, it's best you check the extent and weight of your pocket, especially if it's going to involve money.

Else, doing something you can't finish might just end up diminishing your stock value, thereby, making you lose out in every position. Also, do not mimic or copy other investors as their pocket weight might vary from yours. It worked for them because they have the means to see it through. Now, ask yourself if you have the same means. If you do, then there should be nothing stopping you from implementing the strategies and wanting the best for yourself.

2. Goals of the Investor: It is important to know that some investors don't just want an extra push in growing their investment. As a matter of fact, the investors just want to buy the stock, then leave it there to swell naturally without bothering to lift a finger. Don't get it twisted, some investors can be like that. This kind of investi9buy these stocks to tie down their resources.

Now, you need to ask yourself if you are that kind of investor. If you are not, then implementing ways which should help you swell your investment should be your next line of thought. What are your goals? What are your targets? How bad do you really need to achieve those goals? This factor would influence the extent to which these strategies would work.

3. Risk Management: Not everyone in the stock market can adequately manage risks. Some investors just start panicking at the sign of setbacks and obstacles. As a determined investor who is willing to take cutthroat measures in achieving results, risk shouldn't easily scare you. Instead, it should be a stepping stone toward greatness.

Thus, how well can you manage these risks? If you are that good, then how about tweaking this strength for the benefit of your goal? Some investors also prefer to dodging these risks or not engaging in them entirely. This is also great in the stock business. Nevertheless, your thirst for more success in this line of investment would start seeing you walk through these risks and overcoming them as they come.

With that being said, stock investment and the stock market can be quite foreign to the ears of many people in the world today. In other words, not everyone has an idea of how it works. Initially, I was also blank in this line of investment. Whenever I hear the word stock, my mind starts racing back to vegetables, market stalls, and so much more.

There really is no crime in being ignorant about something. No one knows it all. Gradually, I also began to challenge myself into doing well-detailed research on the subject matter, picking up books as regards the topic, surfing the internet, and so much more. Therefore, you are in the right place to get enlightened. Also, you must not be a stock owner before you know about it. Having this knowledge might just come in handy, especially when you least expect it.

Knowing the basics, corners, and loopholes of this subject matter would really give you an insight into the potential ls surrounding investment. An investment which can be in many forms is quite rewarding and exciting. As a novice, even a few hundred dollars can serve as enough money for investments. Investments are not really like the way "Hollywood" movies had painted it. In these movies, investments are mostly painted as a bourgeois experiment.

For example, with a couple of hundred dollar bills, mutual funds are the best platform to invest in. Here, you would be able to gain instant clearance to a lot of stocks. This would give you more than enough diversification as you stock would not be compressed into one place. Many stock investors don't really know this. They tend to get their stocks from the same source, thereby opening their stocks to risks. What if the source falls? What if it liquidates? What if it folds up? These are important questions we really should ask ourselves.

Often times, an investor might run into a complete loss, irrespective of how he or she tries to overcome the situation. This is because of the wrong choice of stock the investor had bought. So, how do ones really know which stock is perfect and which ones are doomed to fail? Here is how.

First and foremost, you really need to converse yourself with the philosophy and history of the stocks you are about to purchase. Knowing if the company is prone to lose or knows how to maneuver its way out of any risk. This would save you the trouble of falling into deadly traps. Additionally, you need to have a well-detailed plan which would serve as a guide towards buying any stock.

With that being said, getting the best out of our investments is the dream of every investor. As no investor prays to lose his or her investments, so is delving into strategies and ways towards achieving this notion quite important. Now, the question we should ask ourselves is, what are the strategies we can use? When can we employ these strategies? Does anyone of these strategies guarantee good returns? There is only one way to find out.

1.   Value Investing Basics: This is one of the best strategies you can ever employ in reaching the peak of your investment. In a layman language, it simply means purchasing stocks whose value had dropped beyond their original market value. But don't get it twisted, the value investing basics strategy doesn't really entail getting the stocks from small-time companies.

Because they are of underpriced value doesn't mean the stocks should be gotten from newbies companies. Instead, you should patronize the big shots. Sometimes, these big shots also have some level of underpriced stocks for sale. This is more like getting the best offers while paying a small fee in return.

Nevertheless, a stock can only be undervalued when the financial statements are way below its expectations. Sometimes, these fluctuations can be solely caused by the prices set by the market. The financial statements entail lots of indicating factors like the balance sheets, income statements, loss statements, cash flow statements, and so much more.

If all these don't meet up with the expectation, then the stock would only become undervalued. However, there can be a contradiction in the correct predictions of the market prices of stocks. Thus, while making a valuation for a specific stock, there are methods that can be used in this process. For example, the DCF analysis, comparing the prices of companies, and precedent transactions.

With all these, you are sure to be on the right path as regards reaching your peak with your stocks investments. You really should have no fear any longer while trying to make the best out of your investments. Just pursue value investing basics strategy and watch your investment grow. At cheap and affordable prices, you would be able to boost and increase your stocks in no time.

2. Value Investing Long-term: Here, you might want to make sure you have a lot of time to yourself because this strategy can be quite demanding. Although it's quite straightforward, it is also time-consuming, especially if you plan on making good use of it for a long period of time. It is also important to know that this strategy doesn't really take shape as fast as possible.

Don't expect it to produce a result within a short time in case you are in a haste to make profits. Thus, we would advise you to let go of these intentions before delving into it. Therefore, how does the value investing strategy works? The value investing strategy entails purchasing stocks from these big shot companies who are known to have a long history of success and profit. These companies' foundations are also well grounded in the market.

Warren Buffett, who is one of the most intriguing value investors in history had also been known to have employed this strategy in more than one situation. In his words, I quote;

"In the short term, the market is a popularity contest. In the long term, a market is a weighing machine."

That way, the company's stability, and durability is what should be paramount when seeking out where to buy your stock.

3.   Growth Investing: This is a complete opposite of the value investing strategy. It is basically known as the twin of the value investing strategy. It is also a great strategy used by lots of investors (both newbies and experts) when choosing a stock or boosting their already established and purchased stocks.

It is also quite synonymous to the long term status portrayed by the value investing strategy. Here, you would only be buying the stocks of companies that are well grounded, of good history and philosophy, and of reliable growth. These qualities would only serve as the deciding factor before choosing where to get your stocks. This is what we call the Growth Investing strategy.

Investors that employ this strategy mostly tend to focus their attention on young and upcoming companies that are rising fast to the top of the economic ladder. If these young companies show new traits that would mark them out of the rest, then growth investors don't waste time in buying stocks from these companies.

They look for points, tendencies, reports, and statements that had shown that the companies had and is still witnessing a significant amount of growth, profits, and stability. That way, there would be an automatic increase in the prices of your shares, the more these companies get their profits. In other words, the more the profits, the more the prices of your stocks shoot up.

Also, growth investors don't wait for the prices and value of the stocks to go down before purchasing them like the value investors. They may even go ahead to buy the stocks far more than the normal price. The worth of the stock is not what should matter but the gain one would actually get from the stock is what should hold substance.

4.   Fusing both Growth and Value: If employed correctly, this might just be the solution to your problems as a stock investor, especially if you are into a long term investing. If this strategy can work for Warren Buffett, then it will surely work for you too. Instead of using one of the two strategies to buy stocks, why not just use both strategies in buying the stocks?

Both strategies can be quite amazing if employed correctly. Additionally, there is a guarantee that you would not lose out totally even if the market crashes.

One strategy is bound to bring you profits even if the other is causing you loss. Like we said above, the value investing method looks at the undervalued stocks in a company while the growth investing focuses on how well the company is in terms of rapid growth.

The value stock is at its best during the period of economic recovery and plenty. A very good example of where the value stock would thrive is the airline industry. This is a great place for the value stock because of the increasing number of everyday patronage and recovery. On the other hand, the growth stock is perfect for long term bull market.

With that being said, we would now want you to imagine the fusion of both strategies. Amazing, right? The investor would no doubt enjoy much confidence in his or her stocks. There would be a higher level of security as regards the stocks. Returns would be equally high with very minimal risks to be taken. There would be a great opportunity where you can enjoy the maximum level of success as regards your stocks.

In theory, the use of this strategy as regards the purchase of stock would bring the investor a high level of returns and earnings, stability in any form of economic crisis, and a very low level of fluctuations as regards the prices of the stocks.

5.   Passive Index Investing: This is a whole new experience as regards other strategies like the value and growth investing strategies. This strategy got the name passive for no other reason other than the rate of redundancy involved in it. Here, the investor is required to do very little or no work entirely.

How does this strategy work? We would tell you. To begin with, the Index investing strategy focuses on dividing the investor's capital amongst various kinds of shares and equities with the aim of achieving the same level of earnings and returns. According to research, there are just a few other strategies that works better than the Index investing strategy. Little wonder why lots of investors prefer this kind of strategy, especially when engaging in a long term project.

There is no better way to pick individual stocks. The Index investing strategy will help you to properly select the right stock and in no time, profits and earnings would definitely start pouring in. Additionally, it is important to note that this line of strategy also comes with patience and tenacity. Phrases like "the patient dog eat the fattest bone" go with this line of strategy.

6.   General Trading: How about doing everything necessary to reach the peak as regards your stock

investments? And when I say everything, I mean going all out. This can include following the market as it takes shape, cutting every corners and setback, and making moves that would reflect well on your investments on a later date.

As a newbie, this is the first strategy that would come to your head while still trying to wrap up your head in the game. You would want to consult books, internet materials, or even get tips from actual professionals on how to row the stock market boat. Trade in all forms and perspective, so long you get to the Promised Land – being the best at stock investing.

7. Selective Trading: This also works like magic. It involves actual scrutiny. It is important to know that most stock investors out there don't just go about buying every mouth-watering stock they could lay their hands on. Just like, a retail orange seller always takes his or her time while picking out the oranges to buy, so does the stock investor takes his or her time before going all out for stock.

After selectively picking the stocks, these stocks might not make profitable yield within the shortest time, but with time, they would surely come through. Within a year or even less, there are sure to have made a reasonable impact in the market, with the prices and value shooting up automatically.

8. Buying cheap and selling expensive: This is the goal of every businessman, making an enormous profit. No one wants to lose out of a deal or business, especially investors. Before investing in a particular stock, a careful investor would have done his or her homework efficiently so as to avoid future setbacks.

One strategy that may allow you to stand out as an investor is to always seek for cheap and underpriced stocks wherever you might find them. This can be like a security stock which can be very useful in time of need. One good thing about this kind of strategy is that the underpriced stocks have a tendency of rising and this can make it become very expensive. No matter how you look at it, it's a win-win situation.

9. Income strategy: Instead of focusing on the value and growth of the company before buying your shares how about you start thinking along the dividend line? This kind of investors is known as income stock investors. Their goal is to be able to generate an enormous dividend rate at the end of buying a stock. If a stock doesn't add up in this regard, you won't see them at all.

Instead of hugging an opportunity to get stocks from companies that are quite fast in appreciating capital, they go for simple but slow-growing companies that pay dividends and promises a very high yield at the end of each year. A perfect example of the type of companies these set of stock investors go for are the utility companies and real estate companies. Additionally, they are also prominent with buying stocks from companies that are facing economic challenges and the prices of their stock must have been undervalued.

10. GARP strategy: This acronym whose full meaning is Growth At A Reasonable Price is a kind of strategy employed by stock investors to bail them out of their mess. How does GARP work? It's pretty simple. All you need to do is to combine the working factors of both value and growth strategy earlier mentioned, but with the addition of a numerical slant.

In other words, as an investor who is trying to include this particular strategy in your stock investments, all you need to do is to search for well-grounded companies with a well-known history of steady growth, a company whose stock prices are considerably low and affordable even with the success rate of the company, and watch your returns increase as your stock value also skyrocket. This strategy is quite famous with Peter Lynch who was a one-time Fidelity fund worker. He had been able to successfully employ and enjoy the success that came with this strategy.

A very important trick one must learn in this type of strategy is to know exactly when and how to buy stocks. As a GARP practitioner, you should only buy stocks at a time when the returns ratio is considerably lower than the future growth of each stock. This is the reason why the GARP practitioners don't go new well to do companies. They believe their profits diminish the more these companies maintain their high returns.

11. Quality strategy: How about the combination of the three strategies – value, growth, and GARP? Amazing, right? Here, the investor focuses more on the quality of the stock and that of the company. They would be on the hunt for quality companies with a very reasonable stock price. Unlike the GARP whose strategy has stringent rules and relationships like the numerical slant, the quality strategy only focuses on the quality as measured quantitatively. And similar to value investors, they don't only focus on the price and valuation but also building up concerns around future valuation.

These so-called strategies are mostly founded by the father of investing himself, in the person of Benjamin Graham. As an investor, he had no doubt one of the earliest people to focus and shed more light on a stock investment. Rumor has it that Graham is the mentor of Warren Buffett. This should tell you how deeply rooted is this man to stock investment.

In his words as regards the strategies and factors surrounding stock investing, I quote;

"Whether the investor should attempt to buy low and sell high, or whether he should be content to hold sound securities through thick and thin—subject only to the periodic examination of their intrinsic merits— is one of the several choices of policy which the individual must make for himself. Here temperament and the personal situation may well be the determining factors."

Irrespective of what Graham thinks or perceive about stock investing, two things should still stand out – consistency and confidence. Consistency and Confidence in oneself as an investor is the elixir of success in this line of business. You need to always know that you ate doing the right thing even when everything just collapses.

You need to be sure that no matter how hard the setbacks may seem, these strategies when employed properly would sweep them away. Also, stay true to yourself. And remember, consistency is key. Imagine the combination of all these strategies towards your stock investment? The good news is that they go hand in hand are can be easily tweaked alongside one another.

As a big shot in stock investing, instead of just sitting on a chair while waiting for the profits to start pouring in, you can just experiment with some new strategies. After all, you've already made a name for yourself. There is nothing to lose. Thus, you can even create your own strategies which would help in making you achieve your goal just like Warren Buffett and Benjamin Graham.

While other investors might want to invest in short term stock investments, you can break that jinx now that you know what to do and how to go about it. Stake higher and on longer terms, if they work out, they are definitely going to be more fulfilling than the short term investments. Though the short term investing has the tendency to bring up fast profits.

After applying these techniques and strategies, watching your stock grow is the next best thing to do. With time, they will blossom into something valuable. Applying these diverse strategies gives more than enough joy than just leaving the stock to grow by itself. With the recession, economic breakdown, meltdown, and even market crash, these strategies you've already employed would serve as a blocking agent as it would shield and maneuver your stocks through these conditions.

The origin of stock buying in a company can be attributed to the notion that accompanies partial ownership of the establishment. According to a popular belief, if you own stock in a particular company or group of companies, then you have become one of the automatic owners of that establishment or company.

Thus, people now begin to associate themselves more in stock buying. If they can't build or start up a company of their own, they can as well become part of a company's future. Nevertheless, the worth of the stock bought can now be calculated with the company's financial capacity. The level of incoming profits, the income, and the revenue all play a major role in this valuation.

Understanding this level of stock investing gives us a better view of the whole perspective. We would now be able to open our minds to the strategies and techniques revolving around it. We would be able to make appropriate and proper use of these strategies to get amazing and overwhelming results. Daring investors can even blend in more than one strategy to achieve remarkable results.

It is important to know that these strategies are more paper oriented than the everyday practical experiment. These strategies had not really been used much in practical terms and lack enough grounds to claim absolute success. However, those that tried it still had recorded success all through the process.

With these strategies, you can now rule your world as regards stock investing. Instead of relying on unfounded tips or awaiting the crumbs to fall off the tables of stock investing legends, you can also swing into action. Listen, even when you fall, you still need to get up and keep moving till you get to the Promised Land. These stock legends you see now were also newbies. So keep trying and don't give up. Follow and make good use of these strategies. The sky would be your starting point henceforth.

SECTION 6:

Rookie Stock Market Mistakes (& How To Fix Them)

Are you a newbie? A beginner in this line of business? Then you are in the right place for tips and valuable information. The stock market can be very fragile and flexible. One minute, it might be looking all friendly and the next, it's going to start looking complicated. Now, as a newbie with little or no experience at all in this line of investing, you are definitely going to panic.

Many years back, I was also in this line with you. As a beginner, I faced lots of complications and ups and downs in the cause of my journey towards becoming a top-notch investor. Along the line, I started seeing things in a clearer picture. It became dawn on me that the steps and decisions I have been making are actual errors and total mistakes.

According to John Bogle who is the founder of Vanguard Funds, I quote;

"Investing is not nearly as difficult as it looks. Successful investing involves doing a few things right and avoiding serious mistakes."

The idea of going into stock investing is no doubt an amazing idea, especially with the extent of return present in it. Nevertheless, this can only be possible if you don't make any mistakes along the line. But as a beginner, the odds are very high for you to make these silly and severe mistakes. Aside from that, human beings are highly unpredictable, thus, there is always a room for these mistakes no matter how careful we try to be.

Be that as it may, investing in the stock market or buying them from companies out there can is the first step towards being a real-time investor. The main exercise that comes after this purchase is the real deal of stock investing. From trading, exchange, and even purchasing more stocks from reputable companies. Each step that follows comes with more than just knowing what to do. No one can boast of waking up one day and becoming a topnotch stock investor, not even Warren Buffett himself.

Thus, learning how to really make things work in this line of business comes with great patience, dedication, and commitment. The mistakes would definitely come as a beginner. There are bound to be times where you would make the not so good decisions relating to your stocks. This is very normal. There are bound to be repercussions after these unwise decisions and silly mistakes. Accept them as they would make you a better investor in the long run.

As a beginner in this line of business, we tend to be swayed by lots of things. For example, the media, the crowd, the atmosphere, and so much more play a very big part in our relationship with the stock market. This chapter would tell you the common mistakes newbies make. Then, you can watch out for them. Now, let's get to that, shall we?

1.   Trading Too Much: This is one of the common mistakes people make as regards stock investing, especially when things start looking good. As a newbie, there is always a tendency for one to always want to trade more and before you know it, you might have traded more than you can actually handle.

The more these trades happen, the more you end up losing. For example, if you end up investing over $4000 on a long term investment, if the market becomes favorable, you will earn more than enough returns. But if you end up trading more than normal, then your returns might just be clouded with loses. Additionally, the timing should be right. There are perfect times that would surge the return rate, all we need to do is to know when.

2. Ignoring Fees: We would advise you to know the fees of a particular investment fund before making a decision. No matter how little the money can be, you should not give it out to your financial advisor without having a clear knowledge of the fees. Many beginners end up overlooking and ignoring these fees. This is very wrong.

As a matter of fact, this simple mistake could cost you a lot of damage to your investments. We should always pay attention to these fees which range from 0.3 percent to a little over 1.0 percent. Additionally, a lot of experts had been able to show the importance of fees on your investment.

For example, an investor who invests $50000 in a particular investment within a long term period of over 20 years with a return of 4 percent per year is likely to be charged with $80000 on a scale of 1.0 percent fee. In the same vein, on a scale of 0.25, the investment is to be charged with $$110000. Now, the choice is yours to pick between these fees percentages.

3. Putting Investments in the Wrong Accounts: Whenever you plan on trading or making good financial transactions as regards your investments, then we would recommend you to be very careful so that you may not fall into paying taxes for an account to you don't even plan to use in the first place.

Many newbies don't know this. They end up forgetting that if your investments get shared into different accounts, then the tax would be deducted from them. This is a loss on your part as an investor. But, if you are thinking about putting your investments in a taxable account for a long period of time, then you should think towards stocks, mutual funds, and even municipal bonds.

4.   Trying to be clever and cunning: The beginning and end of the stock investment lies with the market. No matter how hard you turn or twist this narrative, the outcome will still be the same. The stock market would still be the deciding factor. Thus, don't try to be funny, cunning or trying to act smart. The more you try, the more you would realize that you can't beat the stock market.

As of 2015, statistics had it that more than 50 percent of active money managers had not been able to overturn their situations. In other words, they couldn't beat the stock market. This is a practical situation as regards stock investment. Therefore, don't even start thinking you can do the impossible. If the experts in this field end up failing, what gives you the assurance that you would beat the stock market?

5. Many beginners don't even have a plan: This is very rampant with newbies in the stock business. They blindly follow the flow of the crowd without having a plan of their own. This clueless attitude of theirs ends up putting their investments in danger with lots of setbacks and obstacles waiting to swallow any struggling investments.

Stock trading or investment is just like every other regular investment out there. One needs a well-detailed plan in order to execute and realize the goals and objectives. This is synonymous to expert investors. They know when to trade. They know when to sit back and watch. They know when to sell off their stock. And they know when to purchase new ones.

These and more are what the experts are quite known for. This way, they would be able to maximize their profit and minimize the loss rate. After all, the goal of every stock investor is to gain enormous profits. Additionally, if the beginner investors have their own plan before starting out as a stock investor, there is a tendency for them to abandon this plan in the long run, especially when they are being faced with the realities of investing.

Not having a plan as a newbie can lead to several things that would put your investment in jeopardy. You would start seeing the stock business as showbiz where the money comes from glamour and glitz. You would now start chasing what is in vogue. In this case, you would now start saying things like "let me not miss out of the great things". Trust me, this is the beginning of failure.

This feeling would only push you towards making a bad investment in the long run. Instead of trusting your own plan and initiative, you would now start following the dictates of this new trend. The major reason why we end up losing out while following this trend is because our timing may be wrong. We might end up delving into this trend when the returns that can be gotten from it has expired. Thus, you should follow your plan if you have one.

6.   Overlooking risk aversion: This is a common mistake made by beginners in the stock investment line. A lot of them get to develop the feeling that they are quite great with managing risks, no matter how severe the risk may be. This is very wrong. There is no shame in going for what suits you. If the risks are too big for you to manage, then you can dodge them by all means necessary.

For example, if you are an investor that doesn't have enough capacity to withstand crazy obstacles and problems that may pop up in the cause of building your stock value, then you can easily pitch your tent with a well-grounded company instead of the newbies that are just building their framework and foundation.

7. Time Horizons helps out a lot: This is one thing many investors out there overlook, especially the newbies. Investing without a time horizon is just like investing without a driving force that would gear you towards being productive. The time horizon would always serve as a reminder to excel in your investments and trading.

For example, if you have a time horizon in the form of a long time frame, let's say sponsoring your sibling from high school to college. You would want to do everything necessary in your power to achieve the best out of your investments. The more the time frame, the more we tend to focus more on the success of our investment.

8. Being helpless without a Stop-Loss Order: This is what shows that one doesn't have what it takes to successfully manage a stock investment. Failure to know what this even means translates into ignorance on our part. It shows we have no plan and makes up helpless completely. Now, what does this mean?

The Stop-Loss Order simply means the procedures and processes put into place for the minimal and complete utilization of loss stopping mechanisms. They put an end to a loss before it becomes a problem and sinks down your investments. Additionally, there is a risk or disadvantage attached to this particular order just as there are benefits tied to it. Even with its disadvantages, a lot of investors still make sure they check in with this mistake before making it.

9.   Allowing the losses accumulate: This is the weakness of every investor, both beginners or experts. If you keep allowing the losses mount before accepting and recouping, you might end up losing the investment as a whole. Great investors are known with their tendency to accept the losses as quickly as possible. This would make them develop their next move as soon as possible.

If the losses start piling up, it would end up paralyzing the investment, especially with one wrong move. In the same vein, this inability to quickly accept and embrace a loss would see the investor to start delaying and procrastinating their actions. Meanwhile, the more the delay, the more the losses keeps accumulating.

10.   Too much Leverage and over exaggeration: Sometimes it might be good to overhype your stock success or investment developments but one mistake newbies do is to keep over exaggerating the margins and figures when it is glaring that their investment is

on a downward slope. That is to say that their investment is failing woefully.

There is a huge possibility that your investments would end up being bad when you overhype them. This might even leave you with a huge debt. This is why we would recommend you don't get too carried away with this strategy. Additionally, we would also recommend that you pay close attention to your investment in case you might want to start using this kind of strategy.

Failure to place close attention on this kind of strategy would only mean that your stocks would go way below their actual value. This is definitely a loss o your own part. If you are not lucky, the company might even end up selling your stock to pay for their losses. Thus, be mild with the use of this strategy.

Don't use it too frequently or even too much. They can be very tempting at most times. Be sure to really understand the steps, dangers, and benefits that come with it. That way, you would be able to curtail and withhold its temptations. Leverage, on the other hand, can be seen as a coin with two shiny sides as regards stock investing.

On one hand, it can help boost the earnings made from reliable trades and on the other hand, it can make losses looks more demeaning when trading unprofitable trades. Additionally, thus leverage can be quite overwhelming for beginners to handle. They sometimes might not be able to wield the power given to them by this leverage properly.

11. Going with the crowd: This is one statement I hate as regards investments. For one to be a successful investor, especially in terms of stock trading, there is a certain feat one must overcome or conquer before reaching this level. There are certain decisions that must be made and followed. There must be actions that must be taken professionally and psychologically.

Being creative and initiating unique innovations are just a few. This can only be achieved by not following the crowd. This can only happen by challenging oneself towards thinking outside the box. When you blindly follow the crowd, you end up doing things that aren't even in your best interest. You would now start thinking along this narrative (If this is what everyone does, then why should I do it differently?).

Going with the crowd comes with its own baggage. Where everyone is facing a major meltdown, you would equally not be left out. As a matter of fact, if you are not well equipped for this meltdown, it might shut you down completely. Additionally, we would advise you to stay unique and diversified. That is the only way to stay on top even as a beginner.

Therefore, as a beginner, learn not to make this mistake. We know moments will come when you find yourself completely blind and inexperienced. Sometimes, you might find yourself lonely and wants to get attached to the current trend. Thus, you are bound to mingle with the crowd, but what we are saying is that you don't follow the crowd blindly.

12. Not doing a well-detailed check: One annoying mistake popularly known with these newbies and beginners is the ability not to conduct well-detailed research about a trade before engaging in it, a company before buying into it, and the stock market before becoming an investor. The period of time one should enter into the stock market is also important.

For example, if you enter into the stock market as an investor during the period of a great recession, there are bound to be a repercussion as a beginner because you definitely lack the confidence and knowledge to sail through this overwhelming situation. Always do your homework well before venturing into something you might regret.

No matter how juicy and tempting the trade or company may be, always do a background check on them. Additionally, you should always be aware of the trends, trading techniques, patterns, and timing before going into it. Even when the feeling is overwhelming, when we can't seem to control our feelings about a particular trade, we shouldn't always forget to do a check on it before starting it up.

Now, what does this research do? They help you know how to better approach a trade. Additionally, research helps us know what we can expect from our investment. It gives us a well-detailed guide and explanation about a particular company. So that way, before investing, you would be in control of your investment. You would also be able to draw out a good plan for our research.

However, when one because a real pro in this line of investing, they become too familiar with the steps, processes, and settings of the stock market. They would be able to forecast, predict, and even determine the outcome of a particular trade way before it starts yielding profits. Be that as it may, as a newbie do not try to emulate such person. Even for them, it wasn't easy before they could reach this stage.

Do your research well and be double sure before you engage in anything that might bring the downfall of your investment before you even begin. The research will be your navigation towards reaching the expert stage. This is the power you have as a newbie. Make good use of it.

13.   Getting involved with unfounded tips: This is very prominent amongst beginners. They tend to stick their ears to the ground for such kind of tips. For example, someone who might be willing to enter into the stock market might hear from a distant cousin that a certain stock can be quite amazing and juicy. They may also add that the stocks are affordable and promise great returns within the shortest time.

Do not fall for this lie and trap. I repeat, do not fall for this lie and trap. They are mostly unfounded with little or no fact attached to it. And when these tips prove to be true, they are certainly not the same as they had been told. You would find out that there are lots of things they kept hidden from you. As a matter of fact, you have been lured to buy stocks that are more or less redundant.

Other big sources of unfounded tips are from social media and television. Generally, the investment professionals use the media houses to advertise and give out unfounded tips, knowing fully well that their web of deceit would definitely catch newbies who are hoping to gain. This is where your research would come in handy.

14.   Overlooking the real picture: There is every tendency that a beginner would be carried away by the trend in the stock market and immediately neglects

the bigger picture. It is important to know that the almighty investor, Peter Lynch had one time made a remark about the bigger picture in stock investment.

In his words, he explained how he had earlier found investing tips and ideas by mere looking at his childhood toys. The brand name is very paramount. The same way people will gladly invest in Coca-Cola is how the brand name holds much importance. Always make sure you see the bigger picture even before others see it.

For example, before the technological revolution came into being, the traditional post office system has been in place. As an investor, buying into this trend would be perfect. However, when the new technological revolution that had brought forth social media, internet, and online platforms where one can easily send and deliver messages as fast as possible came into being, then neglecting this previous trend and jumping on the new one is the best decision.

15.   Being overconfident: As a beginner, you should always know that the feeling of being overconfident would always engulf you no matter how hard you try to hide it. For example, after a single trade as a newbie, every other thing now began falling into place as the earnings and returns start pouring in.

This might be as a result of sheer luck. Just normal luck enjoyed as a result of careful dotting of the I's and crossing the T's. Be that as it may, don't let this get into your head and take the better part of you. You met with sheet luck today doesn't really mean you would meet the same luck next time. It might be a different ball game entirely.

This disease known as overconfidence is a very dangerous and harmful path which would only lead to your downfall. Overconfidence breeds pride and makes one become full of his or herself. That way, he or she would not be able to take lessons, learn new skills, and know new abilities. As a result, there are bound to be failure and meltdown.

Additionally, one important mistake these newbies make is going into day trading without the necessary knowledge and skills to properly execute it. If one is not properly oriented as regards this method of trading, one would definitely lose out. It is important to know that average daily trading comes with lots of financial responsibilities.

This is why it is advisable for the beginners of this line of investment not to even dare venture into this kind of stock investment. As a matter of fact, it is specifically meant for experienced investors. Aside from being financially buoyant, you also need to be extremely knowledgeable about the trend.

You can even go ahead and take courses on day trading. We can't be too careful as regards this kind of trading. Thus, if the financial background is great and readily available, if the processes are intact, if our knowledge about this type of trading is also perfect, then there is nothing stopping us from delving into this type of trading.

16.   Underestimating your skills and knowledge of stock investing: A lot of people have this wrong notion that the stock investment is solely reserved for those with soft hands, fast thinking skills, and intelligent mindset. They believe this kind of investment should only be embarked on by the elite's investors. Thus, they end up shying away without even giving this line of investment a single trial.

Additionally, some people just hold the thought that stock investment is a fickle and feeble investment that must be handled with enough care, intelligence, and smartness. These are attributes they believe aren't imbibed in them. Thus, underestimating and underrating their abilities and knowledge to thrive and survive in this line of investment. This is one mistake people make. It is wrong and totally unacceptable.

To begin with, the stock investment field is not created for a specific set of people. Not for the rich or poor. Not for the young or old. Not for the elite or middle-class. It is in fact for all. For those people who have what it takes to thrive and rise up to the legendary status, as the case may be. This is the blunt truth about this type of investment.

With just picking up a few books about stock investment, surfing the internet for ideas, and drawing out a well-detailed plan, you are surely good to go. You just need to brush yourself up and stay abreast with the recent trend. The rest would surely fall into place. If you have what it takes to be a better investor, then go for it. Don't underestimate and overlook your abilities.

And remember, being rational and practical is the best way to approach any setbacks that you would definitely face. Wherever you feel stuck, you can read more books or seek out help from more experienced investors. That is the best way to stay at the top of your game. It doesn't matter if you are just joining the industry today, so long your plan is great and well cut out, you are good to go.

Section Seven:

Investing Alternatives To The Stock Market

In the previous sections, we did talk about the strategies and techniques one can employ in becoming a topnotch stock investor. In the same vein, we also looked into the common mistakes newbies make in this industry intentionally or unintentionally. However, if these common mistakes can lead to the downfall of one's investment, how best can one avoid or even correct them? This was what the previous chapters delved into.

Be that as it may, this is a whole new chapter with its sole focus on reliable and sustainable alternatives other than investing in the stock market. What are the best available options one can think of aside the stock market? How best can these options be? What are the pros and cons of these alternatives? Do they come with their lapses, loopholes, and setbacks? Or are they really flawless, profitable, and obstacle-free?

For example, a lot of people who would want to go into stock investment but stumbled on new and factual materials where other forms of investments like the real estate, for example, seems to be a little bit advantageous than the stock investment might start developing cold feet. Emotions are definitely going to be ruffled with these people trying to weigh the pros and cons of these forms of investment.

If you are one of those people, then you are in the right place for answers. This section would throw light on the other forms and alternatives to the stock market, thereby, making you have a clear head about each alternative. Nevertheless, finding whichever alternative is better is like finding which ice cream tastes better between chocolate or strawberry flavor. They both taste amazing.

However, it all boils down to your personality and taste. For example, you don't expect someone whose family is a real estate mogul to venture into the stock market while neglecting the real estate management he or she is very familiar with. Sometimes, what we really want lies in us. All we just need to do is to seek answers to some mysterious questions surrounding those wants.

Additionally, making these type of decisions can be very hard in the modern world especially with the recent developments and modernization of the world. In the old settings where the stock market wasn't really of much importance, one would have been very swift and fast in taking a decision between the real estate and stock market. Obviously, 90% of us would go for the real estate investments back then.

But presently, these decisions can be easily made without a proper and sober reflection. The new world order and the rapidly improving industrial revolution and been very influential in the importance of shares and stock. Companies and mega stores like Walmart, Dell, Microsoft, and so much more now make tons of profits which can be said to have easily overpowered the profit one can ever make with a real estate investment. Imagine buying stocks of those companies, amazing, right?

The returns these companies make are amazing. Thus, these decisions can be very confusing at times. Nevertheless, I will help break it down for you. Now, how do we make this happen? It's pretty simple. We will have to briefly explain what we mean by these alternatives. Let's begin, shall we?

Real Estate Vs Stock

What do we mean by real estate? Real estate in simple words means properties or plain land. These properties can be in any form. Therefore, one can invest in this type of investment. You can easily buy and sell lands or properties. It is important to know that most real estate investment would surely cost you money in the long run.

For example, as a real estate investor, if you happen to own a piece of land with little or no development on it, there are still some payments you would have to make in form of taxes and maintenance fees. This would continue till you eventually get someone who would buy the land from you or even lease it.

Additionally, some can even go along in gaining before you eventually start thinking of selling it off. For example, you can lease out or rent out your apartment, building, and so much more for a specific price and agreement between yourself and your tenants. Every month or year, you would always have a smile on your face, knowing fully well that your check must definitely reach your hands.

Real estate investors are always current about any form of properties, so long it would end up becoming profitable. Nevertheless, it is important to know that it's not every time these investors gain or make a profit. Sometimes, they end up losing from a deal that seems almost perfect. Additionally, the power of real estate lies with landlords or investors. They dictate the price, they set the standards and make the rules.

On the other hand, the stock is a different ball game entirely. Instead of owning the company, you can just buy a piece of it. Whatever the company does to make a profit is really none of your concern. What should really concern you as a stock investor is the value of your shares, the profits, and the returns you make from those stocks you own.

This is how the stock investment works. For every share that you own in a company, you are entitled to either profits or loss. It's all depends on the present turnover and financial condition of the company. For example, if you end up buying 30,000 shares in a company with exactly 1,000,000 shares, you automatically own 3 percent of that company. Thus, the profits would be allocated to you as well as the loss.

No matter the kind of company you buy your shares from, be it a music-making company, a megastore, a video game company, an automobile company, an insurance company, and so much more, the procedures still remain the same. As a stockholder, you have the power to make decisions for the company. For example, you can exercise your power by voting the Board of Directors who will oversee the affairs of the company. They will stand in your interest and determine key decisions.

Why you should pick Real Estate ahead Stocks

Real Estate: To begin with, you would agree with me that real estate management and investment are quite popular than the stock investment. Even the illiterates would easily explain their definitely of real estate to their own understand and at the same time would remain stuck when trying to explain stock investing. In other words, not everyone knows what stock investment means.

Secondly, real estate investment comes in physical form and this is what most people would want. For example, no one would believe you are rich unless they saw the extent to which you own physical and properties. This is how traditional the world is. Thus, a lot of people would prefer real estate investment because of this.

Lastly, with real estate, there are low chances of falling into the hands of fraudsters. Since real estate comes in tangible form, it is very hard for fraudsters to easily dupe and scam people. Additionally, one cannot easily run into debt with real estate investment. There are lots of advantages that come with this form of investment. You just need to open your eyes to the possibilities around you.

Cryptocurrency Vs Stock

Cryptocurrency is currently the new trend in the world of investments. When it was first introduced and created by Satoshi Nakamoto in 2009. Ever since it had drawn attention from far and near with constant changes made to it. The first Cryptocurrency ever created wad the Bitcoin. From 2009 to this moment, it's been a prosperous journey for the world of Cryptocurrency as lots of people keep learning and delving into the line of investments daily.

Presently, the going trend of the Cryptocurrency had been quite fluctuating without striking a major balance. Expectations had been high and the return, have really not been encouraging. Nevertheless, making tangible profit or loss in this line of investment solely depends on your abilities to navigate the hurdles, setbacks, and obstacles you may face on the course of trading.

Bitcoin prices had also been generally high. It is as if the more people try to enter this line of investments, the more these prices go up. In other words, the recent increase in the prices of Bitcoins is as a result of the rising interest in the people of the world; both at home and abroad. This is why countries like Japan, Korea, United States, China, Venezuela, and so much more are increasingly pushing a strong agenda towards its citizen's massive involvement in this new trend.

In terms of returns, the Cryptocurrency can be quite amazing with the enormous profit you stand to make from its trading. In the last six years, studies have revealed that the Cryptocurrency has been the only currency to have performed great and made enormous yield than any other currency out there. In other words, it's only a matter of time before the Cryptocurrency renders the normal currency useless.

With every process functioning well, every department working properly, and every necessary network getting stronger, the Cryptocurrency trend can be said to be a much better alternative than any other investment alternatives out there. I will strongly recommend investors to really look into this trend.

On the other hand, stock investing is also not entirely bad when compared to the Cryptocurrency kind of investment. As a matter of fact, it also holds it's own advantages and its edges over the Cryptocurrency trend with lots of reason. If you are already into stock investing, then there is nothing stopping you from being a Cryptocurrency investor. There is no law that says that one cannot diversify his or her investment options.

However, both come with whole new responsibilities. Your abilities to navigate between both swiftly and successfully will determine the rate of returns. According to forecasters, the stocks from the FANG (Facebook, Amazon, Netflix, and Google) won't be able to surpass a 5 years old Bitcoin investment. In other words, if the returns from stocks at Amazon garnered a whopping 342% in a period of 5 years, Netflix garnered over 1000% returns within the same period, and Google made 148% in the same condition, then what a 5 years old Bitcoin investment would make is more than five times the returns of FANG. Cryptocurrency would give a return of over 20,000% within the same period of time.

Why you should pick Cryptocurrency ahead of Stock

Cryptocurrency users no longer have to worry as the long-awaited Decentralized Credit Networks has already taken shape. This is as a result of the amazing makeover and effort poured towards it functioning. Users will be able to get loans, credits, and so much more. This would no doubt change the face of Cryptocurrency as it takes it to the next level. To this effect, Dharma Protocol, Nexo, and Maker DAO are wonderful networks which had proven the effectiveness and validity of the Decentralized Credit Networks.

There is a massive campaign on the sensitization and awareness of the world by the Cryptocurrency Industry. Presently, only the minority are well versed with the running and processes of Cryptocurrency. Thus, there is a crusade in keeping the general public abreast with the Industry, as well as its benefits. That way, even the newbies can transform into legends within the shortest possible time.

Additionally, the Cryptocurrency is created in such a way that your bitcoin is not connected to a central bank or any bank whatsoever. In other words, you can transact your business even without getting interrupted with the long chain of bank authorization and complications. This is what the Cryptocurrency will offer you.

Owning Your Own Business Vs Stock Investing

Often times, we would start thinking about the kind of investment we should enter with the little capital in our hands. We begin to ask ourselves important questions revolving around the kind of investment we would want to go into. This is because we want to be double sure before going fully into such investment. Is it favorable for the newbies? Are the rules and principles cutthroat? Are the risks high? These and more are the questions we begin to ask ourselves.

Mind you, it is very normal to get skeptical while trying to choose the best Investment for us. After all, these investments can be quite juicy and confusing at the same time. The Stock investing, Gold investing, Cryptocurrency, Real Estate Investing, and so much more are quite tantalizing but how about investing your little capital inward? Have you given that a thought?

You can simply throw the capital at your own business and watch it thrive. You can build on your idea and initiative. Swell it till it reaches a successive level. That way, you would also become a business owner, an employer if labor. All you need to do is to brush up your ideas. Establish your customer base. Have a well-detailed plan, and the rest is history.

Mind you, risks and hurdles would definitely come as you embark on the journey of making a name for yourself. But your ability to navigate through these obstacles would determine your level of success. Additionally, you should know that owning a business comes with its own factors. If owning a successful business is that easy, then every Tom, Dick, and Harry would definitely own one today.

However, it requires much more than just having the capital. Investing in yourself is great, but are you ready to face the issues that come with being a newbie in a certain line of business? Investing in a business of your own or in another company (stock) are two sides of the same coin. Both are geared towards one result. Gaining returns and profits.

If you should look at it from a closer view, investing in stocks also means you are investing in your company. In my words above, I had explained the importance of owning a stock. As a stockholder, you are not just giving out capital, you are also owning the company. Thus, that automatically makes you part of the owners of the company with specific rights.

However, you just don't buy into a company blindly. There are specific guidelines and rules that must be met. There are conditions you need to put into place. Plans you need to set in motion. For example, before buying into a company, you should be sure the company is easy to understand and very accessible. You should be able to know the vital points of the company.

You should also have a very good record of the company in both the short term and long term investment. How well can they cope as regards this type of investments? If the answer meets your requirements, then I suggest you go into it. Also, ensure that the company has very stable and efficient management. You won't want to leave your shares in the hands of incompetent people, would you?

The company should also possess and be known for their great profit margin and returns. Big shit companies and mega stores are a very good example of this. You don't expect to always lose out if you invest in companies and mega stores like Walmart, Google, Netflix, Amazon, and so much more. Also, the share value should be relatively affordable before you think of delving into it.

However, if you are capable of buying these shares even at exceedingly high prices, then it's all good. You are definitely going to make your money back with these companies. Even at that, many people still prefer to use their money in any way they dim fit than to give it out in the name of the stock. With lots of corruption and misappropriation that is quite popular in the stock market, many people consider stock investing inappropriate and irresponsible.

Why you should consider starting your own business ahead of stock investing

Don't you just like the feeling of being called a CEO? This is the feeling of owning a business would bring. When you direct and execute objectives in your business, no matter how little, there is always a sense of responsibility that would stay around you. No matter how little the business can be, it is still better than throwing money at some stocks.

When you own a business, you have the sole right to give orders, make decisions, and implement decisions all on your own without the need of consulting anybody. The confidence this kind of feeling would give to you is immeasurable. You are the boss of your own. Nobody will be able to give you an order. The profits and losses are all on your own accord.

Owning your own business gives you freedom. You can choose to make decisions anytime you want to. As a business owner, you can even choose to open your business whenever you want. You can choose to make transactions or just stay dormant. You can choose to do anything unlike the stock investing where you can only influence your stock. If at all you have the right to make decisions, then it's your voting power.

With the high risk involved in this kind of investing, you still stand a chance to make more money than investing in stock. This has been proven over time with lots of studies being carried out ad regards this assumption. With stock investing, the profits made by the company will be divided and shared by every stockholder. But if you own your own business and operate it individually, the profits would be yours alone.

Peer to Peer Lending Vs Stock Investing

Are you searching for a much better alternative to stock investing? Or something that is a little better off the stock investing alternative? Then you really need to check out the Peer to Peer Lending business. Trust me, you would be amazed by the kind of processes, procedures, and features it entails. According to many experts of this type of investing, it is the best invest alternative one can ever find his or herself, with very accommodative conditions for beginners.

Peer to Peer Lending which is popularly known as P2P Lending can be described as an amazing way of making earnings or returns in an orderly and systemized manner. Now, how do you make these earnings you so much wanted? The answer is simple. The P2P Lending system creates a pattern that matches you financially with certain individuals, companies, organizations, and even firms who are in dire need of capital. There is a chance of you knowing your match also.

So, all you need to do is to borrow your much a certain amount for investment without the intervention of a financial institution as an intermediary. In other words, you give out money to people who want to use it to invest in their business for a certain period of time and await your interest afterward. This is the case of them investing your money on your behalf to yield a profit.

One good reason why lots of people are entering into this type of investment is the high rate of earnings involved. Especially within the shortest possible time. The central idea of the P2P is to help people with ideas flourish and lay their hands on the much-needed capital. P2P Lending is a win-win situation for both the borrower and the lender. One gets to invest in his idea and the other gets to make his profits through the fixed interest rate.

The capital reaches the borrowers without having to go through the stress of following stringent rules and regulations. For example, the traditional financial institutions would gladly ask you to sign vital documents, even with your collateral in place. Their interest rate can also be outrageous also. This is why P2P Lending is gaining much popularity in recent times.

The P2P Lending procedures and processes can be completed at the comfort of your home. You really don't need to move a muscle. All you need to do is to visit the website of any reliable P2P Lending organization and fill out the details. That is all it takes to be a borrower or a lender in the Peer to Peer Lending system.

The good news is the Peer to Peer Lending institutions also focuses on long term investment programs. They could establish a lending and borrowing system between two or more people in a long period of time. That way, those with long term projects can even get to execute them without the fear of inadequate capital. With the Peer to Peer Lending institution, the lending power is strong because of the large lending power of the participants. However, the interest rate must also be met accordingly in order to inspire and gear up more people to get involved in the money-making venture.

Now, how do you get qualified? It's simple. Qualification quite differs from the institutions. While some focuses on the credit score of the borrower and income, others focus on the work history and the educational background. Nonetheless, they all follow a very strict rule and are quite skeptical before accepting a member. This is to keep fraudsters and scammers away.

Why you should choose P2P Lending ahead of Stock Investing

They are very flexible and quite easy with no stress at all. Instead of following the normal traditional method of getting a loan with these stressful financial institutions, the P2P Lending institutions offer a much easier and faster alternative. Additionally, the interest that comes with the P2P Lending is quite convincing and they come at the shortest possible time. This interest is fixed. In other words, you don't have to worry about being short even if the borrower runs into a loss.

Gold Vs Stock Investing

Like we all know, one of the most precious and valuable asset ones can ever have right now is the gold. Gold is everywhere we go. Gotten from beneath the soil, cleaned, and refined into lots of things, gold can be said to be part of our lives. While some people wear it as jewelry to adorn themselves, others see it as a very profitable business.

However, before going into this line of business, one would need to secure the highest and tightest security because of its value. Unlike stock which is not tangible, gold can be seen or touched which makes it quite risky as a business. Gold is the most precious yellow metal you will ever find in the whole world.

Its uses are quite numerous which makes it very acceptable generally. Now, imagine finding yourself dealing in Gold? That would be amazing, yeah? Unlike stock that can either increase in value or decrease as the case may be, gold can be quite stubborn in this same vein. Over time, it's value had refused to either increase or decrease. And if at all it increases, then it would slightly make a difference.

As a gold investor, you may likely own the business as a whole. Not many people have the liberty to invest in this kind of business because of its nature, however, the freedom and superiority that comes with owning a gold store are amazing. The value of gold lies in its demand and supply flow. In other words, it hardly even grows.

Why you should choose Gold ahead of Stock Investing

The reason why many people still prefer the gold business to stock investing is because of the way inflation affects the gold venture. The truth is that inflation hardly ever affects gold. When inflation hits the economy and commodities start getting expensive, gold is always left out. Also, the value of gold stays intact without fluctuations. This is a very tangible reason why one should venture into this line of business. Unlike the stock investing where there is always a surge and fall in the value of shares, gold is static.

That wraps it all! With stock investing, you are definitely going to be happy when the earnings start pouring in, but with other alternatives we had just mentioned above, you would come to agree with me that stock market doesn't really give much financial freedom, financial confidence, and financial options.

Thank you for sticking with us this far.

www.ingramcontent.com/pod-product-compliance
Lightning Source LLC
Chambersburg PA
CBHW071327210326
41597CB00015B/1374